ONE ISLAND, ONE OCEAN

OCEAN WATCH AND THE EPIC JOURNEY AROUND THE AMERICAS

Written by Herb McCormick

Photography by David Thoreson

Foreword by David Rockefeller Jr.

Introduction by Captain Mark Schrader

Preface by R. Bryce Seidl

ONE ISLAND, ONE OCEAN

OCEAN WATCH AND THE EPIC JOURNEY AROUND THE AMERICAS

TABLE OF CONTENTS

PART 1   NORTH TO THE ICE

Seattle to Newfoundland via the Arctic Circle and the Northwest Passage

PART 2   THE LONG SLOG SOUTH

Across the equator from the Canadian Maritimes to the Falkland Islands

PART 3 CAPE HORN TO STARBOARD

The triumphant rounding of the Horn; a sobering passage through Patagonia

PART 4 CLOSING THE CIRCLE

A Pacific passage: El Niño, the Baja Bash, the Golden Gate . . . and home

FOREWORD

In the realm of ocean exploration, there are not many "firsts" still to be accomplished. But Mark Schrader has achieved one. He skippered *Ocean Watch* as the first-ever continuous, west-to-east circumnavigation by sail of the American continents. On this epic journey, he invited journalists, educators, and scientists to join him, and together they documented and reported on the condition of the Western Hemisphere's precious ocean systems and the coastal residents who depend upon them.

The mission of *Ocean Watch* began in association with Sailors for the Sea, an organization founded by David Treadway and me in response to the Pew Commission's 2003 report on the declining health of our American waters. Our goal is to convert the recreational users of a valuable resource—in this case, sailors and other boaters who enjoy the ocean and coastal waters—into stewards of it.

In 2006, we asked ourselves what Mark, a veteran solo ocean circumnavigator, could do to help us awaken boaters to the dangerous decline in global ocean health. The answer became an expedition called Around the Americas, accomplished on a 64-foot (20-m) steel cutter named *Ocean Watch*. Through the icy Northwest Passage, around the stormy Cape Horn, and beyond, *Ocean Watch* and her crew of brave reporters traveled 25,000 nautical miles in a little more than a year. *One Island, One Ocean* is the remarkable report of that voyage.

One Island, One Ocean documents the importance of ocean conservation—the very heart of Sailors for the Sea's mission. Fisheries are being shamefully depleted. Coral reefs are being diminished. Plastic and chemical pollutants are clogging and poisoning our life-giving oceans. Ocean acidification is jeopardizing all sea life. We hope that our efforts can, in some small way, help raise awareness of this issue.

—David Rockefeller Jr.

INTRODUCTION

Whether it was doodling on a pad while talking on the phone or sitting in class and looking at a map, for as long ago as I can remember, I've always drawn circles around things that interested me. A long time ago, when the Fourth of July corn was taller than me, I drew a circle on a county map around my parents' Nebraska farm, then packed a lunch, oiled the bike chain, and headed out for a country-road circumnavigation of the family farm. To this day, if I'm interested in learning about something, I draw a circle around it, trying to corral my curiosity and imagination within that boundary. Sometimes the circles are small, sometimes they are big—and sometimes I use them as a path that will lead to an interesting journey.

This book is the story of one such journey. It is clear to anyone paying attention that our climate is changing; our mighty oceans are in poor health; and countless forms of marine and land species are headed for unhappy times at best—and extinction at worst. And, I think it's fair to say, we're not paying enough attention to the causes of these changes. It is clear to the scientists who study the effects we as humans have on our environment that some of our behaviors need to change or entire vital ocean ecosystems will be destroyed forever. Our schools need to raise marine science and ocean-health education to the urgent and important status our present predicament requires. Nothing less than the survival of the oceans—and ultimately the human race—is at stake.

While in Italy on a small boat with friends David Rockefeller Jr. and David Treadway, the conversation turned to ideas on how best to motivate sailors and other direct users of our ocean resources to help change destructive practices and take ownership of the complex issues surrounding ocean health. I was suddenly paying close attention. This was something that needed a circle drawn around it—a big one.

That day in Italy, I heard myself saying to my friends, "Perhaps if we drew a circle around the Americas to highlight the fact that they are an island, surrounded by one ocean, and then used that circle as a path for an extended educational voyage, we could actually raise awareness in meaningful ways and change behavior." The circle suddenly became much bigger, and the Around the Americas voyage was born.

Having the conversations, crafting the idea, and drawing the circle were the easy parts. The doing of it was the challenge. And although any day at sea will present unexpected challenges, thirteen months at sea on a 25,000-nautical-mile course with more than fifty port calls in thirteen countries elevated those challenges to a new level for all of us. Along this route, but at opposite ends of the Earth, were two extraordinarily difficult passages: the Arctic's fabled Northwest Passage and South America's Cape Horn. The boat, the crew, and the shore support for the expedition needed to be as well prepared as possible in order to successfully meet not only those challenges but also other extraordinary events along the way.

Without our partners, contributors, supporters, educators, scientists, and guest crew, our idea would still be just that—an idea. The circle would be just a drawing on a page. But with the support of the core crew of Herb McCormick, David Thoreson, and Dave Logan, along with onboard educators Zeta Strickland and Roxanne Nanninga, oceanographer Michael Reynolds, and more than two dozen other visiting guest crew, we were able to accomplish our mission. Sailor, writer, and friend Herb documented the entire voyage so that we could share our story; photographer, sailor, friend, and fellow Midwesterner David captured extraordinary images of the good, the bad, and the truly magnificent things we saw along the way; and, of utmost importance to all of us with lives at stake, the refit, preparation, and maintenance of our mighty little ship, the S/V *Ocean Watch*, landed on the able shoulders of friend and first mate Dave.

For an expedition of this dimension, our onshore and onboard teams were small, efficient, and absolutely dedicated to our mission. In our view, the ocean deserves nothing less. On behalf of this team, it is my privilege to extend a hearty thank-you to our supporters for making it possible for this voyage to be completed and this story to be told.

—Mark Schrader
Captain of Ocean Watch

PREFACE

The story of *Ocean Watch* and the Around the Americas voyage is a global story, but it is made up of countless small stories—of people, geography, culture, adventure, science, and more. Visionaries David Rockefeller Jr., David Treadway, and Mark Schrader understood that a prerequisite to changing the devastating trends of ocean degradation was a much broader understanding of human dependence on the oceans and our stake in protecting them. With oceans so vast, we simply do not have enough ocean advocates to drive political action or grassroots behavioral change. These men understood that the world of science offers the tools to measure, quantify, and describe the forces degrading the oceans. They understood that science, to be understood and appreciated by general audiences, needed to be presented in ways relevant to local populations. They also understood the power of adventure to capture the attention of people in all cultures. From this was born the Around the Americas expedition—a journey combining adventure, science, and storytelling to awaken broader understandings of our oceans and our dependence on them.

On the surface, this first-ever circumnavigation of the American continents is an adventure story starring a sturdy sailboat, a movie-worthy crew, and a shore-based team of supporters, all fueled by generous donors. From the stark Arctic oceans and their declining ice covers through steaming tropical seas and the challenges of fierce storms in the southern oceans, we found adventure aplenty.

But underlying this expedition is a story important to all 6.5 billion people living on this planet—the story of our dependence on oceans once assumed to be so massive that they could absorb anything we might do to them. Many, many people now know how wrong that assumption was, but few people yet understand what is happening and what can be done about it.

The data is unequivocal. Our oceans are changing, and the changes are all bad from the perspective of human life on the planet.

The effluents of affluence, both chemical and physical, are now visible or measurable in virtually all of the waters of the globe. Growing carbon dioxide in the atmosphere is driving changes in global climate, raising ocean levels as ice caps at our poles melt at accelerating rates and threatening the capacity of habitats to support food production for our growing world population. The carbon dioxide is being absorbed into our seas, making the pH more acidic. This subtle change is degrading the capacity of the oceans to support the biologic community that is the base of the food chain for virtually all marine animals.

A remarkable team was built with a commitment to do what we could to move world attention toward addressing these issues. A crew of four men with extensive marine sailing credentials and a 64-foot (20-m) sailboat were the core. A captain, a first mate, a photographer, and a marine author executed this remarkable thirteen-month, 25,000-nautical-mile voyage. Pacific Science Center in Seattle was enlisted to bring science and education programs to the project. With major help from the University of Washington for analytical equipment, visiting scientists measured ocean and atmospheric conditions and performed other "science of convenience." Onboard educators organized and presented ocean science in ports of call dockside, in schools and communities, with the crew becoming environmental rock stars in port after port. With major press coverage and a Web presence, the voyage touched the minds and hearts of thousands of people in countries around the world.

While the challenges are huge, so is my optimism. The degradation of the oceans is the result of billions of us doing small, largely inadvertent things that in their totality are hugely damaging. The good news is that billions of us making small changes in our lives can also have huge positive influences on the oceans. If we have helped create a growing chorus of voices raising these issues to a level of action at the local, national, and international levels of politics and individual actions, our adventure with a mission will have been well worth it.

—R. BRYCE SEIDL
PRESIDENT AND CEO, PACIFIC SCIENCE CENTER

DIAGRAM OF OCEAN WATCH

The accompanying diagrams depict the sail plan and belowdecks layout for the steel cutter *Ocean Watch*, which underwent a complete refit in Seattle prior to the Around the Americas expedition. The versatile cutter rig employed several headsails (the sails forward of the mast) that were set depending on the wind strength and direction. The mainsail could also be "reefed," or shortened to balance the boat in heavy breeze. Down below, the crew's sleeping quarters were located in the forward and aft sections of the vessel; the central main cabin and workshop served multiple roles, including navigating, cooking, socializing, repairs, and research.

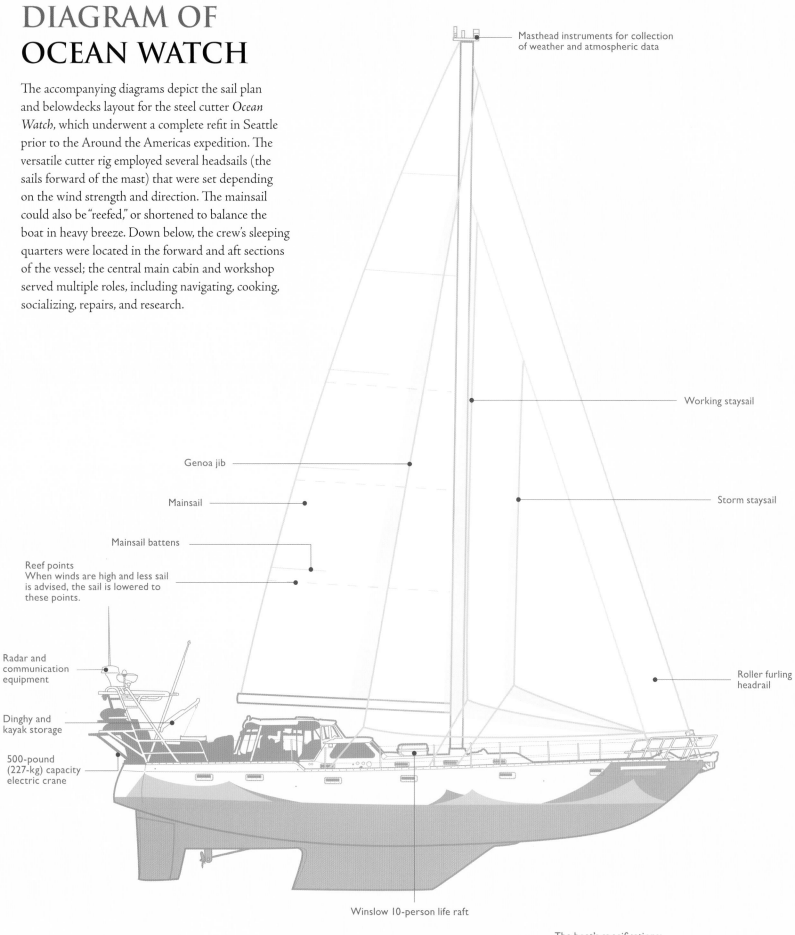

Masthead instruments for collection of weather and atmospheric data

Working staysail

Genoa jib

Storm staysail

Mainsail

Mainsail battens

Reef points
When winds are high and less sail is advised, the sail is lowered to these points.

Radar and communication equipment

Roller furling headrail

Dinghy and kayak storage

500-pound (227-kg) capacity electric crane

Winslow 10-person life raft

The boat's specifications:
Ocean Watch: Bruce Roberts 64-foot (20-m) Pilot House Cutter
Displacement: 44 tons (39 t)
Draft: 9 feet (2.7 m)
Power: Lugger Mariene 135 HP Diesel
Generator: Northern Lights 15 NW
Range (Power): 1,400 nautical miles

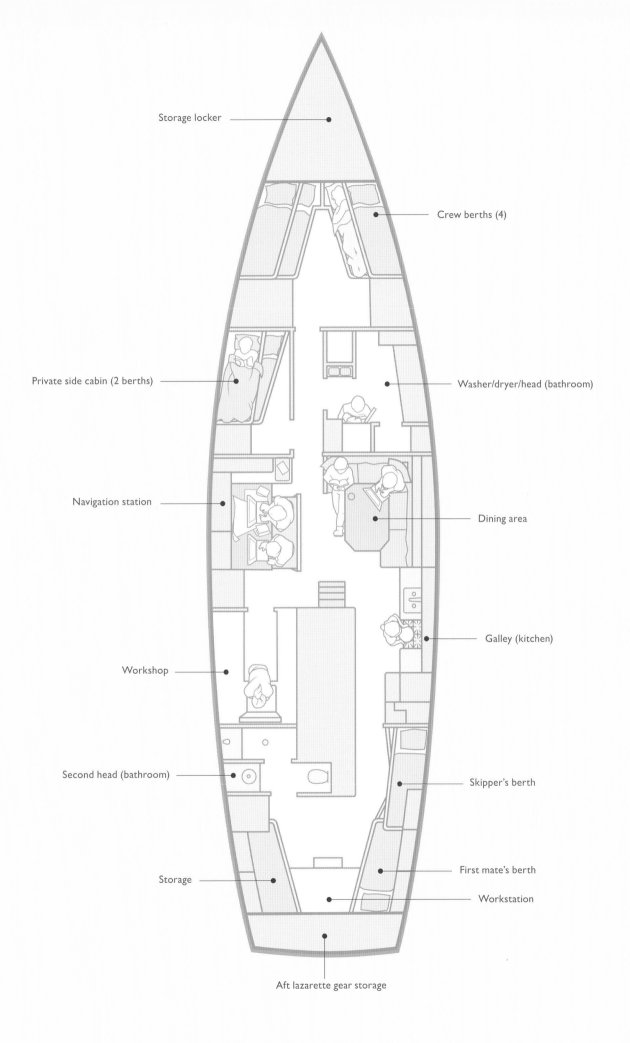

Storage locker

Crew berths (4)

Private side cabin (2 berths)

Washer/dryer/head (bathroom)

Navigation station

Dining area

Galley (kitchen)

Workshop

Second head (bathroom)

Skipper's berth

Storage

First mate's berth

Workstation

Aft lazarette gear storage

St. John's, Canada

Halifax, Canada

San Juan, Puerto Rico

Pond Inlet, Canada

Boston, U.S.

New York, U.S.

Charleston, U.S.

Miami, U.S.

Cambridge Bay,
Canada

Gjoa Haven, Canada

Barrow/
Cooper Island, U.S.

Herschel Island, Canada

Tuktoyaktuk, Canada

Juneau, U.S.

Alert Bay, Canada

Seattle, U.S.

Portland, U.S.

San Francisco, U.S.

Santa Barbara, U.S.

San Diego, U.S.

Puerto Vallarta,
Mexico

Acapulco,

Nome, U.S.

Cabo San Lucas, Mexico

Unalaska/
Dutch Harbor, U.S.

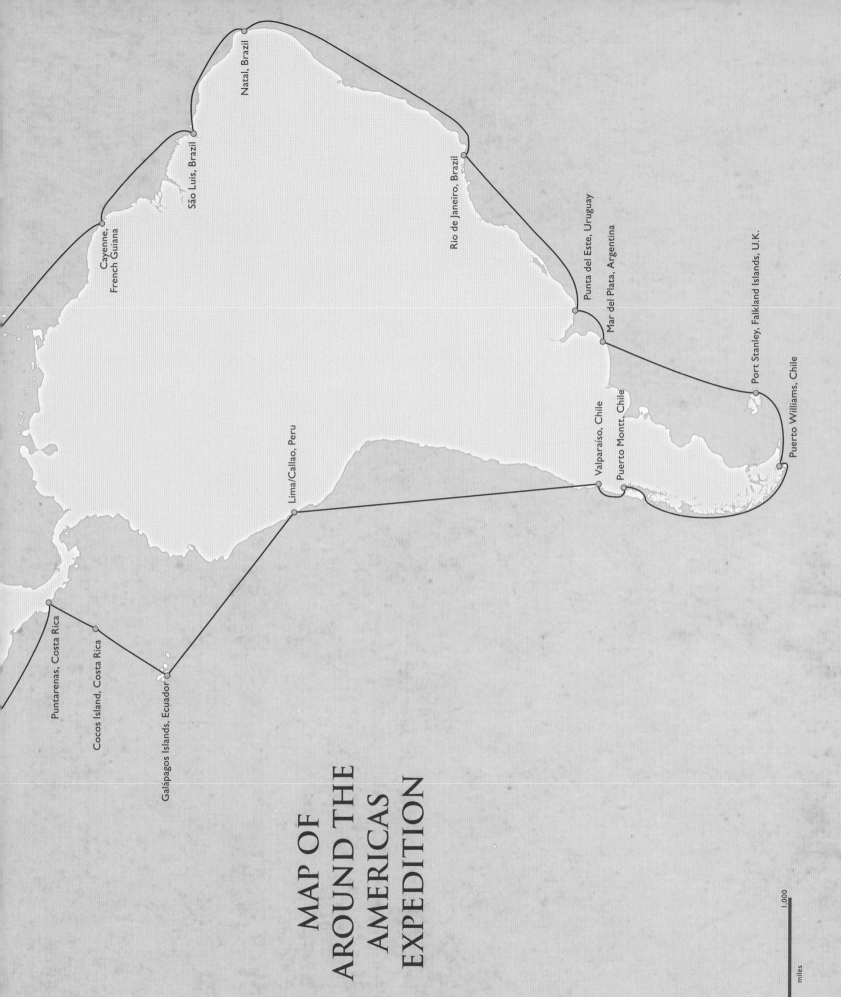

MAP OF
AROUND THE
AMERICAS
EXPEDITION

Natal, Brazil

São Luis, Brazil

Cayenne,
French Guiana

Rio de Janeiro, Brazil

Punta del Este, Uruguay

Mar del Plata, Argentina

Port Stanley, Falkland Islands, U.K.

Puerto Williams, Chile

Valparaíso, Chile

Puerto Montt, Chile

Lima/Callao, Peru

Puntarenas, Costa Rica

Cocos Island, Costa Rica

Galápagos Islands, Ecuador

1,000

0

miles

PART 1

NORTH
TO THE
ICE

CHAPTER 1
FROM THE BIG HOUSE TO THE GHOSTS OF WAR

The spray from the fireboats, celebrating our departure, had long since dissipated, and even the looming presence of Mount Rainier, hovering in the distance beyond the skyline of downtown Seattle, was a memory. Under clear blue skies, on May 31, 2009, the 64-foot (20-m) cutter *Ocean Watch* had set sail from the city's Shilshole Bay Marina, bound first for the nearby seaport of Port Townsend, and then northward for the famed, hazardous, rarefied waters of the Northwest Passage. It was the very outset of the first crucial leg in a proposed 25,000-nautical-mile expedition called Around the Americas. After more than two years of planning and organizing, the voyage had finally begun.

The premise of the trip—a clockwise circumnavigation of the continents of North and South America, from Seattle back to Seattle—was simple and straightforward.

We hoped to demonstrate that the two continents are, in essence, a grand, interconnected isle surrounded by a shared, singular body of water with common challenges, communities, issues, and solutions that link us all together.

One island. One ocean.

This basic premise was clear-cut and uncomplicated. But the execution of our idea, as we would soon come to discover, would turn out to be anything but.

Ocean Watch's core crew—Skipper Mark Schrader, first mate Dave Logan, writer Herb McCormick, photographer David Thoreson, and oceanographer Michael Reynolds—received major backing from philanthropist David Rockefeller's ocean-conservation organization, Sailors for the Sea, and from Seattle's Pacific Science Center. They would be joined along the way by scientists, teachers, and environmentalists. So while the voyage would be an adventure in and of itself, it was based on a mission of science, education, and awareness.

In planning the journey, Schrader realized that the success of the venture would hinge on negotiating two specific bodies of water at opposite ends of the route map. To the north awaited the aforementioned Northwest Passage, an epic, fabled waterway across the Arctic that connects the Pacific and Atlantic Oceans. To the south we would encounter Cape Horn, the legendary waypoint off the tip of South America, positioned smack-dab in the teeth of the wild Southern Ocean. To complicate matters, each had to be traversed during tight, specific, seasonal-weather windows. Schrader had budgeted thirteen months for the voyage; it was a most ambitious timetable.

Schrader referred to the Around the Americas expedition as a "voyage of discovery." After leaving Seattle, the first unsettling discovery was just a few days away.

Above: All for one and one for all (from left): photographer David Thoreson, first mate Dave Logan, writer Herb McCormick, Skipper Mark Schrader, and oceanographer Michael Reynolds composed the expedition's core crew. *Opposite page:* Ocean Watch's first international port of call was Victoria, British Columbia.

THE SALMON DANCE

After a brief visit to Port Townsend and several busy days in Victoria, British Columbia (*Ocean Watch*'s first international port of call), the crew set a course up the Inside Passage, leaving Vancouver Island to port, before making an unscheduled stop at the fishing village of Alert Bay, home to the Namgis Nation. Emily Feffer, an old family friend of the skipper who had worked as a teacher and counselor there for three decades, had told the islanders about our impending arrival. Little did we know, we were about to discover things that would make our hearts soar and sink in equal measure.

The day we arrived turned out to be a special day in town: students at the Alert Bay Elementary School were scheduled to present their annual Cultural Celebration—performing traditional dances passed down through the generations—for the whole community at the "Big House." Not many visitors get a peek inside the Big House—the gathering place for the potlatches, or ceremonial feasts, that are such an important ritual for the coastal Canadian "First Nation" tribes. But Feffer had secured an invitation for us and, astonishingly, we were even the honored guests.

At the outset of the program, Chief William Cranmer acknowledged our presence. "I'd like to welcome our special guests who are here in our house," he said. "They're looking at the oceans to see that we'll continue—or try to continue—looking after our oceans. They arrived here in their big canoe. Will you stand up and be recognized?" We did. And then, sitting back, we were blown away.

Our favorite part of the show was the Salmon Dance, in which first the girls, and then the boys, entered the arena—all in elaborate costume—and proceeded to spin around the fire with joy and precision. "This year," a young girl said by way of introduction, "we've learned about the life cycle of the salmon and what that means. We've learned how important the salmon is to our survival."

Only later, after meeting one of the more remarkable figures we'd encounter on our journey, did the girl's introduction really hit home. The fact that the salmon industry in these parts is in trouble is no secret. But after the presentation, outside the Big House, we met Chief William Wasden, who told a chilling tale about another fish, the torpedo-shaped eulachon (pronounced "yoo-la-kon"), also known as a candlefish.

To the Namgis, and other tribes of the Pacific Northwest, the eulachon is every bit as important as the salmon. For centuries, each spring after the winter melt, Namgis families ventured north to the mainland to harvest the eulachon. The fish is prized for the oil ("grease" in the native parlance) it produces. Boiling the fish to make this grease is a rite of passage, an art that's passed down through the generations. The grease, distributed in big green bottles as gifts at potlatches, is universally revered for its nutritional and medicinal qualities.

The local fishermen have referred to the eulachon as "our sunshine in winter." But due to habitat destruction by industrial logging operations and overfishing as a by-product of shrimp draggers, the eulachon numbers are in sharp decline. Sadly, this wouldn't be the last

Above and opposite page, top: At Alert Bay's Namgis Reservation, we were invited inside the "Big House" for the local elementary school's Cultural Celebration. *Opposite page, bottom:* Afterward, Chief William Wasden explained that the local fishing yields are a shadow of what they used to be.

time on our journey that we would encounter a traditional way of life in serious jeopardy.

Chief Wasden grew up fishing for eulachon. A couple of years ago, after a particularly lean harvest, he witnessed something disturbing.

"Even the animals are wanting," he said. "The eagles are noble. They would never eat our scraps. You can even leave a punt full of fish by the riverside. They'd never touch it. They want it fresh. They want to catch their own.

"But one day, we saw this eagle, eyeing the eulachon scraps. We watched him for about forty-five minutes. He kept edging closer. He was hungry. The other birds were watching him, too. Finally, he went for the dead fish, and then all of these eagles were fighting for them. Even the eagles are losing their pride and dignity."

Wasden's nickname is "Wa," an abbreviation of both his family name and his much-longer native title. It means "river." As the afternoon progressed, Wa took us on a tour of the town's rich U'mista Cultural Centre and talked knowledgeably and passionately about the artifacts, totems, masks, and artwork that were on display.

Those things represented the past. Afterward, sitting on an uncle's fishing boat near *Ocean Watch*'s berth, Wa came around to the present. Alert Bay was different when he was growing up, he told us. Kids had never heard of cocaine or crack. That's no longer the case, but he understands. "The fishing industry is dead," he said. "There's not a lot of opportunity here. You sit around here for a long enough time, and you just want to escape."

Wa remembers when he was thirteen, back in the 1980s, and he spent an afternoon fishing sockeye salmon with his dad. He earned a half-share of the catch, the normal initiation fee for a fisherman's first year on the boat. His dad handed over five grand.

"The harbor was so full of seine boats and gill netters and people looking for crews, because there were just so many boats," he said. "The money was great. The town was booming. People were happy.

"Then, about ten years ago, the fishing industry really started to die," he said. "The fish runs weren't returning. A lot of people were pushed out of the industry. There are probably three boats left that still fish on a regular basis. It's sad to see."

Wa had no sure answers as to why, only some educated guesses.

"A lot has to do with the spawning rivers and streams," he said. "The conditions aren't right. The salmon are real delicate. If their home rivers aren't in proper order, then things aren't going to work. You can see all the bark on the base of the river, because of the logging. They tow the logs down and all the bark settles on the bottom of the river. One of the elders showed me. He said they can't get their eggs into the gravel. Of course the sea lice are killing a lot of the salmon fry, but that's not the only reason. Something's happening in the natural environment."

First Nation people in the Pacific Northwest believe that "modern times" began with a great flood, raged down by the Creator as punishment for humanity's disrespect of the land and the animals that ranged upon it. I wondered if Wa thought we were in for another big lesson.

"With the ozone layer and global warming, it'll probably be that way," he said. "But they say it won't be a flood this time. It'll be something different. Maybe fire."

As *Ocean Watch*'s crew left Alert Bay, we were filled with deep gratitude for the amazing generosity of soul and spirit that we'd encountered, but we were also left with one nagging, unsettling question: Will the Namgis kids still do the Salmon Dance once all the fish are gone?

Top: Ocean Watch enjoyed fine sailing in Alaska's Inside Passage before a layover in the capital city of Juneau, which always has its share of traffic *(opposite page)*. *Above:* As we crossed the Gulf of Alaska, the "twin peaks" of the Shishaldin Volcano and the Isanotski Peaks were stirring sights. *Following page:* Sailing the gulf soon became challenging.

AN ALASKAN WELCOME

A few days later, as *Ocean Watch* motored into Chatham Bay for the final stretch of the run to the Alaskan capital of Juneau, a pod of killer whales appeared off the starboard bow.

The whole crew scrambled on deck. At the helm, first mate Logan had spotted a pair to starboard, but suddenly, with a ripple in the calm sea to port, another pair surfaced. Logan throttled back, and the boat glided to a standstill. Suddenly, still another orca became visible, poking up through the surface of the water about 100 yards (91 m) abeam. Then another trio were spotted astern. We realized we were surrounded by a pod of whales.

Logan killed the engine. After fifty-four straight hours of motoring, the silence was eerie, but welcome. At 55° N now, the sun was still high in the west. Its reflection glowed brightly off the glassy sea. All we could hear were the gentle sighs of the whales and the occasional small splash as they broke the surface. No one said a word. The orcas did all the talking. Half an hour later, a pod of humpbacks cruised by, and, just before midnight, a school of Dall's porpoises began to cavort in the bow wave. Meanwhile, a pair of bald eagles wheeled overhead. It was quite the welcome to Alaska.

Soon after, we glided alongside our berth in downtown Juneau. Originally a Gold Rush town, much of the city's economy today is based on the tens of thousands of visitors who arrive each year on the armada of cruise ships that ply the waters of the Inside Passage and Icy Strait.

Like the tourists, we made the requisite pilgrimage a few miles out of town to the Mendenhall Glacier. Some of us on the *Ocean Watch* crew had seen the glacier fifteen or twenty years earlier, and we found ourselves stunned and concerned to see how far it had receded in the intervening time. But on the voyage ahead of us, vanishing ice would be a constant and recurring theme.

Following a four-day layover in Juneau, *Ocean Watch* set sail on the first significant offshore voyage of the expedition, a 900-nautical-mile passage across the Gulf of Alaska to Dutch Harbor near the island of Unalaska, one of the Aleutian Islands. The long week it took to traverse the gulf proved to be a challenging shakedown, as *Ocean Watch* pounded upwind for most of the journey in a nasty southwesterly that stirred up a lumpy, uncomfortable seaway. But we were rewarded on our approach to the rugged Aleutians with a dawn greeting from a pair of cold, stark volcanic mountains, the Shishaldin Volcano and the Isanotski Peaks—the predominant features of the distant Unimak Island. Fresh sunlight set their respective summits aglow while casting severe shadows on the crags and canyons beneath.

There wasn't much to say, but photographer Thoreson, who captures moods as well as images, put it perfectly.

"It's starting to feel like we're in the North," he said.

Ocean Watch's vast array of scientific and meteorological instrumentation included a SeaKeeper underwater sampling system that pumped seawater aboard and measured water temperature, sea salinity, and pH levels, and dissolved oxygen concentrations. As Earth's atmosphere is exposed to ever-greater levels of carbon dioxide, more and more is absorbed into the ocean, where it's converted to carbonic acid. As we crossed the Gulf of Alaska, which is a primary "sink" for atmospheric carbon, the pH levels dropped to a steady 7.58, down from 8.05, the average figure we'd been recording since departing Seattle. Such a change is all that's required to inflict substantial changes on the sea life below.

DUTCH: TREAT?

We pulled into the port of Dutch Harbor, which holds the distinction of being the number one commercial fishing port in the United States in terms of sheer poundage caught. The rugged outpost had the look and feel of a frontier town.

Dutch Harbor is a company town, and that company is UniSea. (It's also the base for the crab trawlers featured in the television show *The Deadliest Catch*.) Of the four thousand residents at any given time, the majority are UniSea employees. Many have come from distant places like Mexico, the Philippines, and other countries in Southeast Asia.

An article by Frank Kelty titled "Discover Sustainable Fisheries" ran in Dutch Harbor's local visitor's guide, and caught our attention.

"Historically our community has benefited from the rich fishery resources of the Bering Sea," wrote Kelty. "For the past 19 years, Unalaska has been the nation's number one commercial fishing port in terms of pounds landed (800 to 900 million pounds or 3.6 to 4 million kg per year) . . . In 2006, Unalaska broke its own national record with landings of 911 million pounds valued at $165 million." By 2009, however, as Kelty noted, those figures were significantly lower.

Kelty also described the development of the Bering Sea red king crab fishery, which from the 1970s through the early 1980s "changed the character of Unalaska from a quiet village of 400 people to a boomtown." As with the gold rushes of earlier days, many came to Unalaska with dreams of making their fortune. King crab harvest levels climbed from 30 million pounds (13.6 million kg) during the 1970s to 130 million pounds (59 million kg) in 1980.

"Dramatically, however, within a two-year period, the crab resource totally collapsed, sending shockwaves throughout the community and the crabbing industry. . . . It should be noted," Kelty wrote, in an observation about the crab quotas that had been instituted afterward, that "those crab stocks, most likely, were impacted by climatic factors, rather than fishing activity."

The Yukon River chinook salmon was suffering a fate similar to that of the walleye pollock and king crab—runs were so poor that in recent years the river had been closed to commercial fishing—and to that of the Alaskan king salmon, the status of which *Anchorage Daily News* reporter Craig Medred addressed in a June 20, 2009, piece entitled "Gulf of Alaska's Salmon Become Scarce As Ocean Currents Shift."

"A second straight year of weak king salmon returns around the rim of the Gulf of Alaska has state fisheries biologists wondering if they might be staring into the face of a bleak future," Medred reported. "Troubling discussions of PDO—an acronym for something called the Pacific Decadal Oscillation—have been spreading coast-wide as kings come back weak in river after river. Historically, there are indications that geographically widespread weaknesses like these are tied to a shift, or oscillation, in Pacific Ocean currents that causes cooler waters to pool in the Gulf of Alaska."

A previous "cool phase" from 1947 to 1976 "corresponds neatly with the last big crash in king numbers in Cook Inlet," Medred reported. Many fisheries biologists agree that overfishing is part of the problem, but scientist Steven Hare identified climate as a significant factor as well. In the mid-1990s, Hare linked the shifts in Alaskan salmon runs to shifts in ocean-water temperatures and coined the phrase Pacific Decadal Oscillation. Fisheries biologists have been talking about PDO ever since, but it took on a new significance last year after ocean temperatures dipped and many important king runs plummeted.

"The downward trends have only grown worse [in 2009]," said Medred. "The king fishing season should at this moment be in full swing across the region, but faltering returns have forced closures of major Kodiak, Kenai, Susitna, and Copper River waters. And where streams aren't closed, there are still worries.

"Given the spread of faltering runs from Kodiak Island all the way to the Stikine River in Southeast Alaska, fisheries biologists believe they know where things went wrong: 'In the ocean,' more than a dozen said when interviewed this week. The how and why of what went wrong there, however, leaves them scratching their heads."

Above: In the Aleutian Islands, *Ocean Watch* shared dock space with fishing trawlers in the bustling commercial port of Dutch Harbor. *Center:* The crew was moved by a visit to the World War II memorial at Fort Schwatka. *Far right:* The view from Ulakhta Head, towering over the waters of Dutch Harbor, was incredible.

Medred quoted a state researcher named Keith Pahlke, whose confusion about it all was quite succinct: "It's a big black box out there. Things have been wacky."

THE FORGOTTEN BATTLE

The discussion about the disturbing trends in the various fishing fleets wasn't our only moving experience at Dutch Harbor. On the eve of our departure, we piled into a Ford Expedition and drove to the relics of the World War II installation known as Fort Schwatka on the Aleutian Islands, a thousand feet (0.3 km) above the waters at Ulakhta Head. We didn't know we were about to commune with the ghosts of war.

Up in the haunting mist, the place—which today is part of the Aleutian World War II National Historic Area—was still, quiet, and a bit spooky. We got out of the truck and started wandering. It was an engineering marvel, a warren of gun emplacements, barracks, tunnels, pillboxes, and fortresses. It had been built in a year and was meant to withstand 100-mile-per-hour (161-km-per-hour) winds. A sign on a bunker explained that this particular point was the former site of a pair of big guns that could fire a shell some 22 miles (35 km).

The Yanks held the high ground, but maintaining that position proved to be a rugged, difficult duty. Many who served in these islands were sent home sedated, in straightjackets—suffering from an affliction known as the "Aleutian stare." And entire native communities were ripped apart, their villagers sent to internment camps for the duration of the war.

The fortress was built to repel the Japanese, and the Japanese did come. The remote Aleutians were a strategic prize, an important waypoint on the Great Circle shipping route, as well as a possible staging area to launch aerial attacks against the U.S. West Coast.

The Japanese bombers appeared over Dutch Harbor on June 6, 1942. But Dutch was luckier than Pearl Harbor. Roughly three weeks earlier, a coded Japanese message about an impending carrier-launched raid on Unalaska Island had been intercepted in Honolulu. The invading aircraft were repelled by prepared antiaircraft fire.

But the enemy did not return home. Instead, they headed west and landed on the outer islands of Attu and Kiska, where they met little resistance. It was the first and only Japanese occupation of U.S. soil. Historians came to call what happened nearly a year after that invasion of Attu and Kiska the "Forgotten Battle," as it took place during the simultaneous Pacific campaign at Guadalcanal. On May 11, 1943, the operation to recapture Attu began; the U.S. invasion force included a group of native Alaskan scouts called Castner's Cutthroats. The landing, which went uncontested by the Japanese forces as they dug in on higher ground, was conducted in brutal weather. The ensuing battle was a bloodbath, with U.S. forces suffering nearly four thousand casualties. The Japanese army was also decimated.

It all climaxed at Massacre Bay on May 28, when a banzai charge by the remaining Japanese soldiers led to vicious hand-to-hand combat. In the aftermath, U.S. burial teams counted 2,351 dead Japanese troops. Only twenty-eight soldiers were taken prisoner.

Back on Ulakhta Head, the crew of *Ocean Watch* looked out over the breathtaking waters in this faraway corner of America that so few Americans ever see. We were in awe of the vast expanse before us and of the sacrifices made by so many to ensure our freedom to venture to sea, lucky and proud to fly an ensign emblazoned with the stars and stripes. As we climbed back into the truck, an eagle perched on a stump nearby glanced in our direction. Very quietly, we drove into town.

CHAPTER 2

ICE CAPADES

The *Ocean Watch* crew put the hardscrabble Aleutian Island port of Dutch Harbor in our collective rearview mirror, motored into a placid Bering Sea, and laid a course just a degree or two shy of due north for Nome, roughly 680 nautical miles away. The forecast was incredible—a ridge of high pressure had eased over the waters, bringing clear skies and pleasant westerly winds. We knew we were dodging a bullet: the Bering Sea has earned a reputation as one of the planet's nastiest bodies of water. As all sailors know, sometimes it's better to be lucky than good.

Now almost a month into the trip, the crew was beginning to establish a regular onboard routine centered around two main objectives—sailing the boat safely and efficiently and conducting the scientific research and data sampling that was a key mission of the expedition.

A week earlier, we'd received an email from research scientist Mary Beth Decker of Yale University, urging us to keep a sharp eye out for jellyfish. "Your run up 166° W latitude is an area that was particularly dense with jellyfish in the 1990s and hence dubbed Slime Bank," she wrote. "The Bering Sea is teeming with life in the summer. I hope the weather cooperates."

As mentioned, the weather couldn't have been more cooperative, and jellyfish are a particular concern to oceanographers these days. Before the outset of our journey, in Seattle, we were briefed by a scientist who specializes in the study of jellyfish—Dr. Jenny Purcell—who outlined the significance of the gelatinous critters to the scientific community and instructed us in the identification and sampling of species we might encounter.

Jellyfish, as it turns out, are an important harbinger—a barometer, if you will—in gauging the health of the seas. And the squishy fellows had been wreaking havoc over vast, watery terrain. In Japan, a recent run of giant jellies had decimated the fishing industry; closer to home, in the coastal California burg of Morro Bay, jellyfish caused a nuclear power plant to close by clogging the saltwater intake tubes. In the Bering Sea in recent years, the jellyfish population has increased tenfold.

As the breeze disappeared a couple of days into the passage to Nome, *Ocean Watch* drifted to a complete stop, and sure enough, we spotted a jellyfish—and then another, and another still. Back in Dutch Harbor, we'd met fisheries experts who explained that the walleye pollock catch in the Bering Sea was significantly down the previous year. The precise cause remains a mystery. It's one of the reasons Purcell had

Above: As we sailed north above the Arctic Circle, whale sightings were welcome and common, but the challenges presented by the ubiquitous pack ice (*opposite page*) were far less appealing.

28 ONE ISLAND, ONE OCEAN

enlisted us in her studies. Could these jellyfish help scientists discover an answer? Or, perhaps, could they somehow be the cause?

NOME SWEET NOME

Just before midnight on the last day of June, precisely on schedule, *Ocean Watch* motored into the dusty, historic city of Nome after a largely uneventful passage from the Aleutians. The sun was still high in the west. Outside the breakwater, a couple of hopeful gold prospectors were drifting over the calm waters in their rather dilapidated dredges, visions of a new address on Easy Street dancing in their heads. Nome was founded during the original Alaska gold rush, and a new one had begun. All sorts of prospectors had landed here and set up shop, on vessels ranging from the sublime to the ridiculous.

For the next week, Nome served as our base camp as we began to seriously focus on our attempt at the icy and dangerous Northwest Passage. Meanwhile, we took the time to savor a unique and singular slice of Americana—Nome's fleeting, funky Fourth of July parade—and learned some things about the place's fascinating history.

The gunslinger Wyatt Earp was cooling his heels in Yuma, Arizona, in 1897 when he first heard word that there were golden fortunes for the digging in the wild territory to the far north. It took Earp a good two years to actually get to Nome, and when he did, he found a way to bolster his bank account without running up against the law. Earp's saloon, the Dexter, attracted a larger-than-life clientele every bit as formidable as the proprietor: the writers Jack London and Rex Beach; prizefighter Jack Dempsey; and a brilliant mining engineer named Herbert Hoover, who was destined for renown in another arena.

THE VANISHING BARRIER ISLAND OF SHISHMAREF HAS BEEN DESCRIBED AS "THE MOST EXTREME EXAMPLE OF GLOBAL WARMING ON THE PLANET."

Earp was long gone by the time Norwegian adventurer Roald Amundsen sailed into Nome in 1906 after a three-year odyssey aboard his ship, the *Gjoa*, becoming the first skipper to successfully negotiate the Northwest Passage. But the mere mention of Amundsen refocused our energies to the task at hand.

Specifically, we started to think long and hard about ice.

In 2007, Thoreson and the crew aboard Roger Swanson's *Cloud Nine* had negotiated the passage from east to west in shocking, unheard-of fashion: that summer, the Arctic had experienced a catastrophic, record-setting loss of sea ice, and the fiberglass 57-foot (17-m) boat transited the famous northern waterway totally unscathed, never touching a single patch of ice. And *Cloud Nine* had company, as three other yachts also made it through successfully. The 2008 season brought more of the same, as another seven small boats bagged the once impassable Northwest Passage in nearly ice-free waters.

But there are no givens at any time above the Arctic Circle, and from the outset of our travels north, it was clear that, in terms of cold and ice, 2009 was going to be a more challenging year than the previous two. The preceding winter and spring had both been significantly colder, and the new sea ice had combined with old floes that had broken free from the ice cap in 2007 and 2008 to form serious choke points at several significant junctures along the Northwest Passage.

"Patience," said Thoreson, again and again. "We'll need to be patient. We won't decide when we can move. The ice will."

All that was readily apparent by studying the excellent ice charts published regularly by the Canadian Ice Service, which we downloaded and pored over on a daily basis. Up north, the open-water "leads" through the ice had yet to appear. Clearly, we had a long summer ahead.

Above: Due to rising seas, melting permafrost, and warmer temperatures, the remote Alaskan village of Shishmaref is crumbling into the sea.

BOUND FOR BARROW

For the most part, however, it appeared to be clear sailing from Nome to our next major port of call: Barrow, Alaska. At 71° N longitude, Barrow is the northernmost city in the United States and would serve as our entryway to the Northwest Passage. To reach it, we needed to cover roughly 450 nautical miles via the Bering Strait and the Bering and Chukchi Seas.

Along with Christopher Columbus, George Vancouver, James Cook, and so many others, Captain-Commander Vitus Jonassen Bering of the Russia Imperial Navy was one of the grand explorers in what may be considered the great age of discovery. During the course of two major expeditions in the early- to mid-1700s, Bering greatly expanded the Russian empire from Siberia to North America, pioneered the geography of the North Pacific Ocean, and laid the groundwork for Russian trade and settlement in the American West.

On July 8, in a significant milestone on our own voyage of discovery, the crew of *Ocean Watch* successfully transited the 50-mile (80-km) strait that bears Bering's name. It was cold, drizzly, windy, and daunting—in other words, precisely what we expected. As crazy as it sounds, we wouldn't have wanted to pass the Bering Strait in any other weather.

Into the Bering Sea we sailed, ticking off miles at a steady 9 knots. We hadn't previously had a real taste of the Bering—we'd motored almost all the way from Dutch Harbor to Nome—but we now found ourselves sitting down to a banquet. *Ocean Watch* seemed pleased with the circumstances; some of the crew, their stomachs churning, were less enthused. Trucking along on a close reach into sloppy beam seas, the motion was lively, though the scenery was just the opposite. The low profile of the Seward Peninsula looked like an inside-out Dalmatian—a long expanse of black ridge freckled with countless white splotches of snow. Lots of words came to mind, none of them floral bouquets. Rather: *Nasty. Bleak. Unforgiving. Ridiculous.*

On we sailed.

Visibility was limited, which was a shame. In one of her more famous proclamations, ex-Alaskan governor Sarah Palin once said that you could see Russia from her homeland. We knew that if such a view was ever going to happen for us, today would be the day. The Russian island of Big Diomede was some 20 nautical miles to port, with Siberia another 25 beyond. Sadly, we never caught a glimpse of either.

By midafternoon we were abeam of Cape Prince of Wales, which was only 5 nautical miles away, but we couldn't see it. The cape is the line of demarcation between the Bering Sea to the south and the Chukchi Sea to the north—in other words, it's smack-dab in the middle of the Bering Strait. On deck, you could see smoky breath in the chilly air. In the previous four hours, the water temperature had dropped from 52° Fahrenheit (11° C) to 42° F (6° C). A fair current of up to 3 knots was scooting us on our way. At the change of watch, the fresh crew showed up on deck swathed in multiple layers of clothing.

An hour later, the cape and the Bering Sea were behind us. The next significant waypoint was the Arctic Circle itself. As it turned out, we had one more dangerous hurdle to clear before passing it.

THE TOWN THAT'S MELTING AWAY

Just a few nautical miles south of the Arctic Circle, which begins at 66°30' N, we set a course for the tiny Alaskan community of Shishmaref on the very exposed northwest coast of the Seward Peninsula, a place we were all very curious to see. A week earlier, a BBC reporter had visited the place and described it thusly: "It is thought to be the most extreme example of global warming on the planet." We didn't detour to Shishmaref because it was a boomtown. Rather, it's a town going boom.

A double-barrel combination of rising seas and melting tundra is what's causing the tenuous barrier island on which the town of Shishmaref was built (more than four hundred years ago) to slowly vanish. During the last three decades, temperatures have risen in the Arctic, and the permafrost is thawing.

Combined with the northerly winter gales, particularly at times of high tidal surge, the northern shore of Shishmaref is crumbling and being claimed by the sea. Some locals estimate that the erosion is occurring at a rate of about 3 to 5 feet (1–1.5 m) per year; others guess the figure is close to 10 feet (3 m) a year.

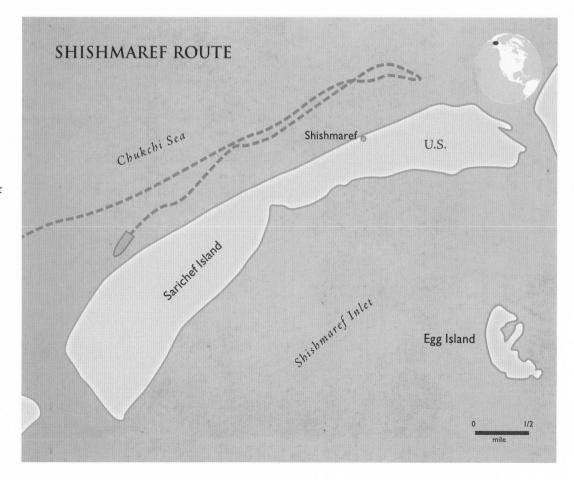

SHISHMAREF ROUTE

Chukchi Sea

Shishmaref

U.S.

Sarichef Island

Shishmaref Inlet

Egg Island

0   1/2
mile

Right: This graphic shows the path of *Ocean Watch*'s approach to Shishmaref. When the boat went hard aground, the crew sought a winding escape route back to the open sea.

BERING STRAIT ROUTE

RUSSIA

Ualon Lagoon

Chukchi Sea

Pooten Bay Cape Peek

Shishmaref

Big Diomede Island (RUSSIA)

Little Diomede Island (U.S.)

Ikpek Lagoon

Cape Nunyamo

Lopp Lagoon

Bering Strait

Wales

U.S.

Port Clarence

0   15
miles

Details. Either way, Shishmaref is disappearing. We wanted to witness it for ourselves, and we got close enough to view numerous homes and buildings sliding into the sea. But the approach to the low-lying isle is poorly marked, making navigation difficult. The surrounding waters are shallow, and *Ocean Watch* draws 9 feet (3 m). And so, on a dark night, in a rising breeze, on a lee shore, we inadvertently went aground.

Luckily, helmsman Dave Logan's quick actions thwarted catastrophe, and *Ocean Watch* bounced and bumped her way into deeper water with her steel hull intact, relatively unscathed. We didn't dare a second approach.

Still, we'd seen enough to understand that the forces of nature are blasting the place with double-barrel intensity. "The waves are larger because there is no sea ice to diminish their intensity, slamming against the west and northern shores of Alaska, causing severe storm-driven coastal erosion," said Patricia Cochran, the executive director of the Alaska Native Science Commission. "Permafrost is melting all over Alaska as a result of rising temperature, causing land underneath many villages to subside and softening the soil on riverbanks like the mighty Yukon."

In his story about Shishmaref, the BBC's Bryan Willis quoted Professor Gunter Weller, the director of the University of Alaska's Center for Global Change and Arctic System Research, on several points. "Shishmaref is an indication of what to expect in the future in other parts of the world," said Weller. "In that respect, it is the canary in the coal mine." Willis concluded his piece on an ominous note, calling "the people of Shishmaref the first refugees of global warming."

From the shallow bay, we could see evidence that the people of Shishmaref had waged a serious battle with the forces of nature, specifically with the rugged seawall they erected in an attempt to fortify the very foundation of their town and their life. But it's not enough, and the islanders know it: the community had already begun searching for a place to relocate.

Aboard *Ocean Watch*, once the adrenaline had stopped pumping, and as we sailed away from Shishmaref, we couldn't help glancing over our shoulders. It's a sight we'll never again see. For in all likelihood, we won't pass this way again. And even if we do, the town called Shishmaref probably won't be here anymore.

INTO THE ICE

After our nerve-wracking grounding off Shishmaref, we stopped for a couple of days in an idyllic anchorage in Ledyard Bay to sit out a passing gale and collect ourselves. Once the front had passed, the weather was gorgeous, and some of the crew broke out the sea kayaks to explore the coastline, while others took the dinghy into shore.

The melting tundra was squishy beneath our sea boots, but after several days at sea, it felt great to stretch our legs. From the boat, the permafrost had been a wide expanse of brown and green, but treading upon it, we were treated to a zillion miniature gardens of delicate florets, in endless varieties of shapes and color. After the gray trip north from Nome, the soothing blues and violets and pinks and lavenders were gloriously hypnotic. It couldn't have been better, and then it was: low evening sun blinked free from the clouds and washed the entire scene—flowers, valleys, hills, and snow—in clear, brilliant, radiant light.

Too soon, we were underway again. But as it turned out, we'd been wise to refresh and recharge our psychic batteries.

Thirty-odd hours later, on the first day we encountered the northern pack ice, the morning had started harmlessly enough. By 7:30 AM, on an errand for the scientists back at the University of Washington's Applied Physics Lab, we'd retrieved a previously deployed weather buoy that had drifted ashore on a low barrier island, thus

Opposite page: Luckily, *Ocean Watch* enjoyed superb sailing conditions heading north through the Bering Strait, and the fine weather continued during a layover in Ledyard Bay (*above*).
Following pages: On the approach to Barrow, Alaska, *Ocean Watch* encountered the ice pack, prompting Skipper Mark Schrader to scout for safe leads.

accomplishing our good deed for the day. Closing in on 70° N, Barrow was less than 80 nautical miles away.

A couple of hours later, someone on the foredeck made what at the time seemed like an innocent-enough remark: "Hey, there's our first ice!" It was a long, low expanse of pack ice, still a few nautical miles away, and if you didn't put much thought behind it, the stuff looked no more threatening than a tempting stretch of white-sand beach.

Shortly thereafter, a spotter plane from the National Oceanic and Atmospheric Administration (NOAA) flew overhead on a routine mission, and their findings, if anything, confirmed our misguided and soon-to-be realigned notions that the day ahead would be a stroll in the park. Yes, they confirmed, there was ice ahead; they reported the

weapon, who on his third trip to the Arctic had probably forgotten more about the ice than the rest of us would ever know—was hoisted up the rig to scout safe leads through the floes, brash, and bergs.

Captain Schrader was on the bow, waving his arms like a traffic cop at rush hour in a busy intersection. First mate Logan had the helm, weaving the 44-ton (39-t) cutter though the frozen waters like a skier negotiating a steep pitch, always seeking the path of least resistance.

The ice was ubiquitous, and seemed to represent every possible size, shape, and description.

One rather flat ice table was inhabited by a sleepy slew of walrus; another hosted a resident confab of murres, standing upright like penguins, in a committee meeting with no end in sight.

coordinates for the open leads between the ice, and we dutifully jotted them down. All we had to do was connect the dots. "See you in Barrow," they said.

But then we came upon the ice quickly, and the previous reassurances from the long-gone NOAA pilot offered little or no relief. Though we would eventually learn to negotiate the northern pack ice with a modicum of grace and efficiency, and to identify and follow leads through the ice mazes while skirting the impassable blockades and logjams, in this inaugural encounter, our collective familiarity with ice-strewn waters was minimal.

Two hours later, we were more or less surrounded by ice. With camera and binoculars in tow, photographer Thoreson—our secret

We missed most of the ice, but not all of it. That would have been an impossible task. Making contact with ice is an interesting experience. The first time you do it, you're terrified. The second time, less so. The third time, it's like, "Okay, whatever."

In these perilous conditions, we were lucky to have a quarter-inch steel hull on our side. The dangerous bergs were the ones that appeared innocuous, a pretty ice sculpture above the water—"Hey, that looks like a rabbit!"—but with a deep, ponderous keel below: an upside-down toadstool of ice.

After a while, we were out of the worst of it—or so we thought. Barrow was 25 nautical miles ahead. The coastline was spectacular. "Look," someone called, "there's the marker showing the site where the

Above: On the final miles to Point Barrow, herds of caribou sauntered along the nearby shoreline. *Opposite page:* Once there, the crew discovered a vibrant scientific community and seized the moment by taking a hike through the tundra with a researcher studying the effects of the changing permafrost.

plane bearing Will Rogers went down in 1935! And up on that ridge, a herd of caribou. Check out the antler rack, silhouetted against that blue, blue sky."

Then: More ice. Lots more ice. Thoreson went back up the rig. Schrader returned to the bow. It was a maze of ice, a field of ice, a riddle of ice. Logan cut inside toward shore. At one point, the depth sounder recorded 11 feet (3 m) of water under our keel; *Ocean Watch* draws 9 feet (2.5 m). He took a deep breath and kept steering. The closer we got to Barrow, the more entrapped we seemed to be. Fortuitously, we'd sailed into the high latitudes and the land of the midnight sun, where the perpetual summer daylight made piloting much easier.

Even off the small town of Barrow, however, it turned out that the

No, it was a floating iceberg, the size of a Hummer, firmly ensconced on our anchor chain. It wasn't the first drifting floe we'd fended away in the ripping current. That's when the shout came from shore, in a distinct Inuit accent. It bore a succinct message that got our full, undivided attention:

"The ice is coming in. Your boat will sink in ten hours."

We absorbed that nugget for about a microsecond: Your boat will sink in ten hours.

"You know," someone said, "he might be right."

Up came the anchor and *Ocean Watch* was once again a going concern, this time bound for a low spit of land that serves as the outer boundary of an ice-choked bay called Elson Lagoon, a few miles north of the actual town of Barrow.

ice was nearly onshore, and the loud reports from the rifles of the seal hunters working the nearby floes seemed like a fitting soundtrack.

But well after midnight, more than ten hours into our "ice capades," we dropped the hook off the open roadstead by the village's main drag and everyone took a few deep breaths.

We thought we were okay. In fact, half the crew retreated to the cockpit for a fortifying beverage, celebrating what we thought was the end of one of the more exciting, harrowing, adrenaline pumping, exhausting days of our sailing lives. But our respite was short.

For the other half of *Ocean Watch*'s crew were on the bow, long lances in hand, a trio of Queequegs fighting off the Great White Beast. Only this white menace wasn't Moby-Dick, and those weren't harpoons.

For the second time, the anchor chain rattled down and the hook was firmly set in about 15 feet (5 m) of water.

There was ice off to the east of us, ice to the west of us, and ice in the lagoon directly ahead of us as well. But *Ocean Watch* was lying in an expanse of clear blue water, and as near as we could tell, we were safely positioned in an ideal location for the southwesterly breezes that were forecast to roll in.

Even so, if we'd learned anything during that endless day, it was that our thoughtful, logical assumptions regarding ice—and how to deal with it—were about as solid as mist.

But for the moment, the drama was over. We'd survived, and so had *Ocean Watch*. Our next big bout with the ice would come another day.

CHAPTER 3
THE BIOLOGIST, THE HUNTER, AND THE BIRDMAN

Some 330 miles (531 km) north of the Arctic Circle and less than 1,200 miles (1,931 km) from the North Pole, the roughly four thousand people in Barrow, Alaska—including the largest Inupiat Inuit, or Eskimo, community in Alaska and one of the largest in North America—often refer to their settlement as the Top of the World. This also happens to be the name of the rather ramshackle, two-story blue hotel on the main drag. The inn does a brisk summer business with tourists anxious to catch a glimpse of the famed midnight sun.

Barrow is the namesake of one John Barrow, a secretary in the British Admiralty, who in 1816 launched what's been called the most ambitious program of exploration ever. These journeys did not always end well. It was Barrow who dispatched Sir John Franklin on his ill-fated search for the Northwest Passage, a deadly errand that resulted in the loss of 128 men and two ships and became history's longest and least successful search-and-rescue operation.

Ocean Watch's first attempt at anchoring off Barrow brought to mind what in retrospect was certainly a poor choice of names for one of Franklin's ships: *Terror*. After a local advised us that we were in imminent danger of sinking, we sought a safer anchorage outside of town. We anchored there for three days until the ice cleared and then returned to our initial anchorage closer to town.

As the largest city in Alaska's North Slope Borough, Barrow is today a vibrant crossroads for Arctic scientists and researchers who venture to the high latitudes on all manner of projects and studies, many of them in concert with the fascinating Barrow Arctic Science Consortium (BASC). One of them, snowy owl expert Denver Holt, invited us on a hike to have a look at the fluffy white birds.

"The snowy owl is a 'key species' in the Arctic ecosystem," Holt explained. "By bringing attention to the life of the snowy owl, I hope to also bring awareness to the plight of other species and the delicate balance that exists in the Arctic as the climate changes."

We'd planned on spending a week in Barrow, but that notion turned out to be wildly optimistic, as the ice to our immediate east in the Beaufort Sea remained a formidable (and impenetrable) presence through much of July. As it turned out, our forced layover presented the opportunity to meet some fantastic people, including a pair of men who, at first glance, seemed like the unlikeliest of colleagues, never mind friends.

Their tale begins in 1977. Fearful that the bowhead whales of the Western Arctic were in serious jeopardy, the International Whaling Commission (IWC) took forceful measures by issuing a moratorium on commercial and subsistence whaling. The Eskimos, who for centuries had relied on the annual bowhead hunts for survival, were up in arms.

Above: Barrow, Alaska, the northernmost city in the United States, is some 330 miles (531 km) above the Arctic Circle and a long way from . . . everywhere. *Opposite page:* During the two-week visit, *Ocean Watch* anchored off the open roadstead just off of town.

Historically, the Bering Sea had been rewarding grounds for whalers. The famed Nantucket whalers of New England discovered the whales in the mid-1800s, and in 1852, at the height of the bowhead hunt, some two hundred whaling ships plied the waters near the Bering Strait. In 1849, more than 1,700 bowheads were captured, and 1852 proved to be a record year with some 2,188 captures. By the tail end of the commercial whaling trade, in 1915, only 1,000 to 1,500 animals remained. Though Eskimos continued to hunt whales on a subsistence basis, the bowheads began to make a slow recovery.

Then, in the late 1960s and early 1970s, the oil pipeline hit, and suddenly Barrow had a lot of cash. At the same time, a resurgence in traditional Native American culture and practices took hold. Suddenly, instead of inheriting all the equipment, as had always been the case, young whale hunters could buy all the gear they needed to. So the numbers of crews increased and so did the harvest levels.

That's when the IWC intervened, believing the bowhead population to be in free fall, with no more than 1,500 animals in existence. The Eskimos, who'd been observing the whales for centuries, believed the estimates were far short of the true figures; based on that claim, they were able to negotiate a small annual quota to continue the hunt until a reliable count on the bowhead population could be established. The federal government had funding in place to try and get a firm grasp on the numbers, but it was small consolation to the hunters and their families, who relied on the bowheads for survival.

STRANGE BEDFELLOWS

Into this maelstrom stepped a young scientist named Craig George. Hailing from Wyoming, George's knowledge of bowhead whales and the natives whose lives depended on them was virtually nonexistent. However, he soon met a local subsistence whaling captain named Harry Brower Jr., and the alliance they forged is a story worthy of Hollywood.

These days, Brower and George work together for the North Slope Department of Wildlife Management—but their relationship was hardly cordial at the outset. After all, Brower's job was killing whales, and George's job was counting them.

Harry Brower Jr.'s grandfather, Charles D. Brower, was a legendary Yankee whaler who settled in Barrow and married an Eskimo woman. Harry's father—Harry Brower Sr.—became the head of the carpentry shop at the Naval Arctic Research Laboratory (NARL). He was also a hunter and a guide, and in that capacity he became an invaluable resource and a fount of local knowledge for the NARL scientists, making countless contributions to their research. In that regard, Harry Jr. was destined to follow in his father's footsteps.

Today, some whalers not only pilot an umiak—the light, shallow-draft skin boats that have been used in the Arctic for centuries—but also command an office, and Brower's is located on the campus of Ilisagvik College. (Not coincidentally, Craig George's office is right next door.) When you ask Brower to describe his occupation, he speaks more to the essence of *who* he is than *what* he is.

"I'm a hunter," Brower said. "I did a lot of fishing, hunting, and trapping with my father when I was growing up. It was the tail end of the dog-team era." Like all Eskimo kids back then, he started out as a companion to his father and grew into an apprentice. In the winter, he helped set and retrieve the trap lines for Arctic fox. In the spring and fall, he and his father went after the grandest prize of all: the bowhead whale.

"It was all part of our livelihood," said Brower. "It was the subsistence way of living." He harbored no ambition to captain a whaleboat. He'd started whaling when he was young, with his uncle and cousins. The hunt was never about the whales alone—it was about family and community. But inevitably, the generational torch was handed down. It was time, urged a cousin, for him to get his own crew, on his own boat.

"You can be your own captain," said the cousin.

"Oh, man, you can't put me in that situation," said Brower. But when Craig George walked into his life, his destiny was sealed.

Craig George remembers vividly his first days in Barrow, over three decades ago. "There were some very unhappy people here, to say the least," he recalled. "At least a two-thousand-year whaling history had—boom—come to an end. It was a tense situation. You can imagine there were some choice expletives when they saw a white biologist walking down the street."

And then there were the whales themselves. "I didn't even know what a bowhead was," he said. "All my training had been in terrestrial biology. Very little was known about the whales scientifically; they were poorly described. So I didn't understand the animals. And I didn't understand the waters. I just started writing things down."

He also set out upon the pack ice, into the wild of the unforgiving Arctic. "It's a dynamic environment, where the local hunters are really on their game," he said. "They know when it's safe, when it isn't, when the pack ice is going to come in, when the leads are going to open and the whales are going to migrate through.

"So we started going out there and counting whales. We learned from the hunters how to cut trail through the pressure ridges, how to put camps in, how to deal with the polar bears, all that sort of thing. It took a

Clockwise from opposite page: Barrow's "skyline" is negligible, and polar bears wander its outskirts. For recreation, the crew played soccer on the high-school field and took a hike with renowned musher and wildlife biologist Geoff Carroll.

UNLIKE THE GRAND BANKS COD FISHERY, THE BARROW "BOWHEAD PROJECT" IS ONE OF OCEAN CONSERVATION'S TRUE SUCCESS STORIES.

long time. Initially, I was more interested in the logistics and the camping. And I started to see that it really is very beautiful on the ice. In a weird way it sort of filled my need to be in mountain country."

With guidance and support from the Browers and other hunters, George and his associates gained knowledge and understanding. Though they disagreed with the actual numbers, the Eskimos who'd been fishing for decades acknowledged that there were problems with hunting and that the bountiful population of bowheads had, in fact, dwindled.

"Once we started to really work together, that's when things started to really take off scientifically," George said. The Eskimos began to tell him things that, at first, seemed difficult to believe. "They watched us observing the whales and said, 'You're not doing this right. You're only counting what you can see. There are whales out there you can't see, in the offshore leads, and when it's frozen they're still swimming right through here.' That was a little hard to accept at the time.

"Sure enough, they were right," said George. "We began to track them acoustically and realized that thousands of bowheads can move under a complete ice cover. They crack the ice and punch holes in it so they can breathe. Anything less than a foot thick seems pretty transparent. And once one whale breaks through, other whales will find these holes and use them. It's just amazing. Over the course of the day, hundreds of whales can use one of the holes."

Beyond observing the whales, the hunters allowed George to conduct post-mortem examinations. Not long ago, he discovered the fragment of a Yankee whaling weapon, patented in 1879, embedded in the scapula of a captured bowhead. There's little doubt that it struck the whale more than a hundred years ago: the life span of a bowhead can be 150 years or more.

During the course of his career, Craig George has made other important discoveries. "It turns out, the hunters were right in the beginning," he said. "The early estimates of a thousand whales turned out to be around four thousand. It took us a decade to figure it out and show that was the case. It's been a win-win deal. We believe the population is somewhere around twelve thousand bowheads, and it's increasing. The collaboration with locals is very important. I look around at other wildlife and fisheries management regimes that aren't in it together; they're separated and even in conflict, and it's their resources that are often in greatest trouble. Your North Atlantic cod fishery is a good example of where things went horribly wrong. The science was ignored. It was a perfect storm of how not to manage a resource.

"But when biologists and users walk side by side, good things happen. I think the Bowhead Project is a perfect example and, arguably, one of the great conservation success stories of the last century. The Eskimos who hunt bowheads believe you can't catch a whale unless you've done so with honor, dignity, and respect. A whale, it's been said, will offer itself to a worthy hunter. It's called "the gift of the whale."

George has earned his own gift from the bowheads. "The animal has really given me a lot," he said. "Kind of a life focus: direction in many ways. And they're just incredibly interesting. They're really outliers in the mammalian spectrum in a lot of respects.

"We're doing pretty well," he said and then smiled. "I say 'we.' I'm not a bowhead." Craig George may not be a bowhead. But like his mate, Harry Brower, he's just completely, and totally, at one with them.

The collaboration between biologist Craig George *(top)* and whaler Harry Brower Jr. *(bottom)*, as well as other scientists and hunters, secured the future of the once-endangered bowhead whale. ***Opposite page:*** A bowhead whale tail is seen against the backdrop of Barrow.

FOR THE BIRDS

Eventually, the ice leads to the east began to appear, and a few hours after *Ocean Watch* left Barrow, the tiny barrier island called Cooper hove into view. Cooper Island wasn't on our original itinerary, but we'd been asked to deliver supplies to ornithologist George Divoky, who has called the island home each summer for the last thirty-three years.

Cooper is roughly the width of a football field and about three flat miles (5 km) long, situated hard by the gray Beaufort Sea. Once *Ocean Watch* was about a mile off the beach, we could make out three silhouettes, in descending order of stature: the pair of lonely towers for the wind generator and weather instruments, respectively; the rickety ex-storage shed that serves as Divoky's seasonal homestead; and Divoky.

The fact that Divoky, who stands about 6 feet (2 m) tall, was the third most prominent feature on the Cooper skyline speaks volumes.

Strapped to his back was his rifle, a Cooper fashion accessory that wasn't at all necessary back in the 1970s but that has become essential since the turn of the millennium, when polar bears began arriving.

We dropped the hook well offshore in a choppy seaway and deployed the dinghy. Swathed in foul-weather gear, Dave Logan, David Thoreson, and I set out for the lonely figure waving from the beach.

Divoky has given much of his professional career to the black guillemot. He knows more about this tough and tender Arctic seabird than anyone in the rest of the world ever will. He first set foot on Cooper Island in 1972 as a twenty-six-year-old ornithologist, while working for the Smithsonian Institution in a study to identify and document vulnerable seabird habitats. The island was littered with abandoned 55-gallon (208-l) oil drums and empty ammunition boxes left by the U.S. Navy after the Korean War.

In a 2002 cover story for the *New York Times Sunday Magazine*, author Darcy Frey described what happened next: "Two black guillemots, startled by the crunch of gravel, suddenly flew out from beneath an ammo box. Since guillemots don't normally breed in this part of the Arctic, it was, in Divoky's words, 'definitely a hit.' He looked around and found eight more pairs breeding in the boxes, at which point, he says, 'I almost wet my pants.'"

It was three years before Divoky returned to the island, where he found eighteen pairs of guillemots breeding in the boxes. In an attempt to expand the colony, he began creating new nest sites.

By 1978, 70 guillemots resided on Cooper Island; in 1981, the population had risen to 220. Nine years later, almost 600 birds called Cooper their summer home. "For many years," continued Frey, Divoky "pursued a rather esoteric study of them—mate selection, age of first

breeding. . . . Then, almost by accident, he discovered that his birds were picking up on another kind of frequency, and that if he watched and listened with great care, they could tell him about something no less consequential than the climatic fate of Earth.

"In 1995, in response to Vice President Al Gore's task force on climate change, a call went out for data sets: did anyone have information that would shed light on regional climate change? Divoky acquired National Weather Service data on when the snow melted at Barrow and plotted the dates on a graph.

"Then he looked at his own data on when the first egg showed up on Cooper Island and plotted those dates as well. The correlation leapt off the page: from 1975 to 1995, snow was melting in northern Alaska, on average, five days earlier each decade. Over those same twenty years, the date his guillemots laid their eggs was occurring, on average, five days earlier each decade."

Divoky knew that guillemots required eighty snow-free days of summer to mate and hatch their chicks, and that there were few snow-free spans of such duration until the 1960s. The conclusion was obvious: in two short decades, the short Arctic summer was arriving ten days earlier. And it was having a biological effect, noted Frey, by "leaving a fingerprint on a species living in a seemingly remote, pristine environment thousands of miles away from the industrial hand of man."

OF BEARS AND PUFFINS

Quite unexpectedly, Divoky's studies of black guillemots morphed into a definitive statement about one effect of climate change at the apex of the planet. Receding pack ice, melting permafrost, and the arrival of a new species of predators and competitors, the horned puffins, are all contributing to the guillemot's not-so-well-being.

Fluffy black guillemot chicks (*top*) have drawn ornithologist George Divoky (*bottom left*) to remote Cooper Island for more than three decades. The recent arrival of polar bears (*above*) has forced him to abandon his tents for more secure shelter (*opposite page*).

But for the scientist and his subjects, the biggest new problems, literally, are those polar bears.

"From 1975 to 2002, I saw one bear on this island," he said. "Since 2002, they've been here every year. And last year, they were here every day for my last week on the island, a different bear each day." The reason is simple. The pack ice that for nearly three decades was within sight of Cooper—and the big, fat, abundant, blubber-coated seals on which they feasted—was now nowhere in view. The bears are hungry. They're swimming to Cooper Island in search of chow.

For the first twenty-seven of his thirty-three years on Cooper, Divoky camped in a series of tents, but with the arrival of the bears, he'd hauled an old shed to the island for shelter. As we walked up to it, he told us the tale of his latest unwanted visitor, who'd shown up a week earlier and worked his way up the beach, flipping over nest boxes and eating the chicks before swimming away.

"I mean, people ask me if I believe in climate change," said Divoky. "And I say, 'No, but I believe in polar bears.' When I see a polar bear, I know that's a polar bear. But I also know I was out here for so long, and I didn't see polar bears. So, you know, something's going on."

Polar bears aren't the only change that's come to Cooper. "Since 2003," he said, "there have been more puffins on the islands, and puffins have killed more and more chicks. One year, we had 180 chicks after hatching took place. Sixty of those were killed by puffins, and sixty of them starved to death because the ice was so far offshore and there was no real good alternative prey." And then there's the island itself. "All the freshwater ponds have disappeared because they lost the ice under them. So the whole island is changing while things are changing offshore."

There used to be well over two hundred functioning guillemot nests on Cooper Island. The day before our visit, after the latest polar bear rampage, there were eighty-five. So, one had to ask: How many more years, George? How long will you keep coming back to Cooper?

"I came here to see how this seabird could react to different prey abundance and species types in terms of raising their young. That's not really possible now when the puffins are coming and killing the chicks, and the polar bears are flipping over their nest sites. So I think the puffins and polar bears will decide when this really isn't worth my time. If the thousandth bear is the one that's going to get you, I'm up to some level now, so I don't want to be around when the 999th comes strolling down the beach. I'm trying to avoid that."

So, Cooper Island without George Divoky? Like the cold, bleak world around him, it's hard to grasp. Like the changing Arctic itself, it just wouldn't be the same.

CHAPTER 4
A NORTHWEST PASSAGE

For centuries, beginning shortly after Christopher Columbus's inaugural voyage, European navigators set forth across the Atlantic in search of a direct, all-water passage—a Northwest Passage—that would link Europe to the Orient and bypass the long, hazardous routes around Africa's Cape of Good Hope or South America's notorious Cape Horn. The rewards for the sailors' discovery of a shorter, more efficient trading route through the Arctic from the Atlantic to the Pacific, strictly by sea, would be many.

It wasn't until 1907, however, that a stubborn Norwegian explorer named Roald Amundsen accomplished the feat after a three-year odyssey aboard his specially built, 72-foot (22-m) sloop, *Gjoa* (pronounced "jo-ah"). Although successful, Amundsen's difficult transit clearly demonstrated that the waterway held little mercantile appeal. Even so, the challenges the route presented would prove to be compelling and irresistible to many mariners and adventurers.

In the following century, roughly a hundred boats completed the journey, with about 70 to 75 percent of them being icebreakers or ice-reinforced vessels. The first "modern" cruising sailor to navigate it was a tenacious Dutchman named Willy de Roos, in 1977.

Now, aboard *Ocean Watch*, it was our turn to have a go. After our brief interlude on Cooper Island, we were finally heading eastward, but progress came in fits and starts. We made our first call in the Canadian Arctic at the old whaling camp on Herschel Island, the tiny dot teetering atop the pillar of the *i* that represents the vast Yukon Territory on the mainland directly to the south. It had taken seven weeks to negotiate our eventful travels around the perimeter of the remarkable state of Alaska.

Sir John Franklin, the leader of a deadly expedition that would bear his name, was the first European to visit this island, and he named it after the English astronomer and chemist, Sir John Frederick William Herschel. From 1890 to the early 1900s, a succession of whaling ships, having exhausted the inventory just about everywhere else, used Herschel Island as their base of operations in the final throes of the whale trade.

Today Herschel Island is a Canadian Territorial Park, and we ventured ashore to take in the sights. Among these were an old outpost of the Hudson Trading Company; the missionary's home (which was at one time insulated from floor to ceiling in Bibles); and the bone and baleen house, which doubled as a makeshift courthouse.

Afterward, as a pair of caribou wandered along the bumpy dirt airstrip, we strolled into the boggy terrain and paid our respects at gravesites commemorating the short lives of several whalers who plied these waters a hundred years ago. For those unfortunate few, Herschel was their final harbor, their last port of call. Thankfully, it wasn't ours.

Above: Bleached antlers lie in the foreground of the historic whaling station on Herschel Island in the Yukon Territory. *Opposite page:* While on the island, Skipper Mark Schrader paid his respects to the whalers who never returned home.

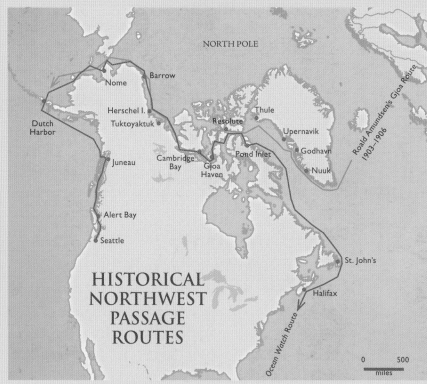

HISTORICAL NORTHWEST PASSAGE ROUTES

RETURN TO THE ICE

As we scanned the ice charts on the first of August, it was apparent that several key roadblocks loomed ahead in the form of at least three major waterways still choked with ice. Arctic veteran David Thoreson's early advice invoking patience while waiting for safe leads to open water became our mantra.

After an overnight stay off Herschel Island, we called in at the clean and orderly hamlet of Tuktoyaktuk (also known simply as "Tuk"), the first of several planned stops in the small Inuit villages dotting the sprawling Canadian wilderness known as Nunavut. Entering the winding channel with charted depths of a mere 12 feet (4 m) was nerve-wracking, but the scenery was sensational. The Tuktoyaktuk Peninsula is world-renowned for the 1,350 pingos—hills of solid ice covered by a thin layer of soil and insulating plants—scattered off its coastline.

During our visit to Tuk we got a glimpse of traditional subsistence living from local fisherman Wayne Thrasher before again pushing onward through Amundsen Gulf to a remote mainland anchorage called Pearce Point Harbour, where progress came to a crashing halt for several days due to another serious blockade of pack ice directly in our path.

Our French friends aboard the yacht *Baloum Gwen* soon joined us, and via the radio we learned the crew of another boat we'd met in Barrow, the 40-foot (12-m) Canadian sailboat *Silent Sound*, was in a nearby anchorage. Like *Ocean Watch*, the other pair of boats was attempting a rare west-to-east Northwest Passage run. We were surprised in Pearce Point to learn about a fourth vessel undergoing a westward attempt, a tiny 17-foot (5-m) open boat sailed by a couple of intrepid British Royal Marines.

On August 13, after thoroughly exploring the beaches and scenery at Pearce Point, we raised the anchor and resumed our voyage out of the Amundsen Gulf and into a relatively narrow waterway called the Dolphin and Union Strait. For almost the entire summer, this slim

passage flanking the southwestern coastline of formidable Victoria Island had been jammed with ice. Finally, the ice charts revealed a hint of a lead opening right along the Victoria shoreline. Holding a heading just north of east, we made good progress throughout the day.

As the evening progressed, though, the ice became more formidable. Ice concentrations are listed in tenths: 0/10 means ice free, 10/10 means completely solid ice. From his position back up the rig, Thoreson estimated that *Ocean Watch* was negotiating anywhere from 2/10 to 4/10, all the way up to 6/10 of ice. The latter is a serious patch of ice.

We made good progress right through the gorgeous pastel sunset, just before midnight, but by 1:30 AM visibility became difficult. The refracted "mirage" of ice on the horizon looked five stories tall, so we shut the engine down for about three hours while the boat drifted to the northwest, in company with the pack ice, still making almost a full knot.

The sun rose a little before 5 AM local time, and we resumed progress. Our long-lost old friend, the moon above, had reentered our lives. As we eased back into the floe, the moon, about half full, was reflected in the windows of icy film that represented the interface of the new morning air and the cold Arctic Sea. We were cruising through slush.

After a winding tour of the ice maze, we made landfall off Cape Baring on Victoria's big knuckle of land, the Wollaston Peninsula, and closed to within an eighth of a mile of shore before finally hanging a hard left-hand turn and making our way to the relatively clear corridor of open water along the coast. And I do mean relative: we still faced ice aplenty. Negotiating these hazardous waters was a total team effort, with ice spotters in the cockpit, on the bow, and occasionally aloft, feeding the helmsman a constant stream of information as we slid to the east.

The next night, we were stunned when our VHF radio crackled to life and, soon enough, we could see the source of the transmission: Major Tony Lancashire and Lt. Col. Kevin Oliver, of the British Royal Marines, and their diminutive sailboat, moored to an ice floe close to an otherwise barren and exposed shore. We launched our dinghy and brought them aboard *Ocean Watch* for hot drinks and heard they were on an "adventure training" holiday between tours in Afghanistan.

A day later, after a winding forty-eight-hour tour through the maze of ice, *Ocean Watch* finally broke free into beautiful, welcome blue seas and continued on to the next significant destination, the village of Cambridge Bay. It had been two and a half months since departing Seattle, and the ship's log read 4,876 nautical miles.

From Cambridge Bay, it was another 230 nautical miles to Gjoa Haven. The first half of the trip was uneventful. Outbound through the open waters of Queen Maud Gulf, *Ocean Watch* enjoyed ideal sailing conditions until the wind increased to a steady 25 to 28 knots, and we reduced sail and resumed motor sailing. But the final hours into Gjoa were tense as we wound our way through two roughly 30-nautical-mile sections of water littered with rocks, shallows, and low-lying islands. The second stretch, a zigzagging waterway called Simpson Strait, was

probably the most hazardous we'd seen since leaving Seattle. And we entered Gjoa Haven in the dead of the dark, ever-lengthening night. But Amundsen himself once called the protected anchorage the "finest in the world," and when we awoke the next morning and had our first real glimpse of the surroundings, it was hard to disagree.

IN AMUNDSEN'S WAKE

After breakfast, we had a stroll through Gjoa Haven and saw numerous references to Amundsen on plaques and in a tribute to him in the village's administration building. Amundsen was different from many of the highbrow explorers who preceded him, many of whom perished tragically. By embracing local language and culture, engaging in the first real trade with the natives, and more or less showing respect for the elements and wildlife on which their lives depended, Amundsen blazed a new trail that extended beyond the course he set or the route he established. It's fitting the place was named Gjoa Haven.

Opposite page: For centuries, explorers searched for a waterway from Europe to the Far East, but Roald Amundsen was the first to establish a Northwest Passage route. *This page, clockwise from top left:* In Pearce Point Harbour, the crew discovered bear tracks, enjoyed a campfire with the crew of *Baloum Gwen*, investigated a cairn left by earlier explorers, and admired a bearded seal. *Following pages:* The Arctic twilight was always mesmerizing.

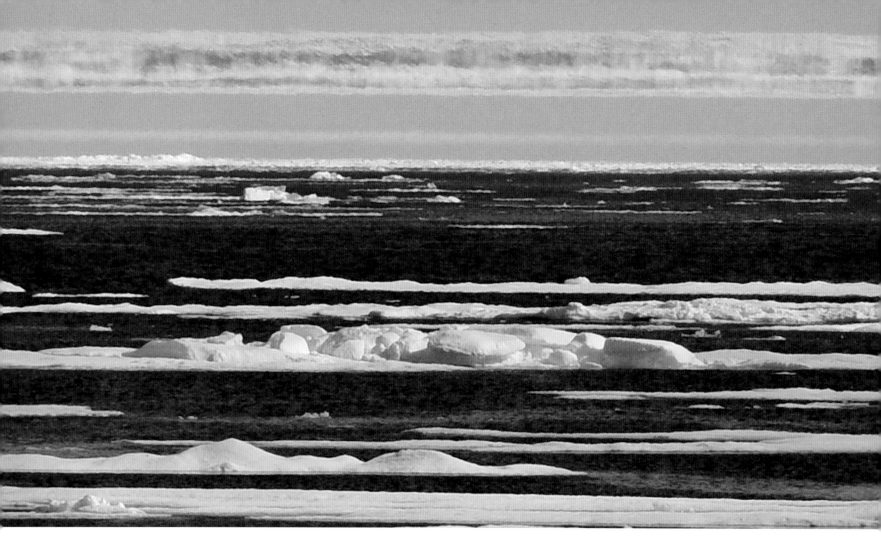

During our stay in Gjoa, the captain of the Canadian Coast Guard icebreaker *Sir Wilfrid Laurier* invited us—and the sailors from *Baloum Gwen* and *Silent Sound*—for lunch and a briefing on the weather and ice. We were all especially interested to hear the latest regarding the long finger of water to the north called Peel Sound, historically the "make or break" section of the Northwest Passage. For months we'd been obsessing over that sound, the primary obstacle on the Arctic voyage. Over the years, many a crew had found themselves trapped for the winter, their boats icebound, after failing to negotiate Peel Sound.

In the two previous years, the sound opened up in mid-August, and small yachts like ours sailed through with ease. The story was different in 2009. Old ice to the north that had been dislodged that spring had mixed in with new ice in Peel to form a rather imposing barrier to safe navigation. On the *Wilfrid Laurier*, ice expert Bruno Barrette's forecast was almost too good to be true. A massive high-pressure system had parked over Peel. With relatively warm temperatures and little wind, Barrette was confident Peel would soon be passable. An ideal weather window had opened.

The time to push forth into the hazardous, icy seas north of Gjoa—Larsen Sound, Franklin Strait, and Peel Sound—was now. In spirit and execution, we approached this crucial leg like mountaineers on a final sprint, after weeks of staging, from base camp to summit. The sense of urgency aboard was palpable.

After leaving Gjoa, we spent a night anchored in Oscar Bay on the west side of Boothia Peninsula. From there, we motored northeast into James Ross Strait and onward to Peel Sound. Our original itinerary called for us to continue north around the top of Somerset Island to the town of Resolute. However, on the southern side of Somerset was a noticeable 19-nautical-mile shortcut called Bellot Strait, which would shave many exposed miles of potentially icy waters off our journey. The trouble was, Bellot usually is, and appeared to be, clogged with ice.

For much of the next 100 nautical miles, we steered hard to port, then hard to starboard, this way and that, through a significant maze of pack ice. Following one last, edgy stretch through the thickest ice we'd seen in weeks, *Ocean Watch* made it to the mouth of Bellot Strait. A few hours later, Skipper Mark Schrader described the experience in his personal log, beginning with: "We're out!" He continued:

> After a pretty harrowing morning navigating through fog, heavy ice concentrations (not shown on our ice charts), two polar bears (mom and yearling cub) on a small floe, and rocky shorelines, we made it to the west entrance of Bellot Strait. We arrived about an hour later than the Arctic Sailing Directions recommended for riding a fair, safe current. As we approached the entrance to Bellot the ice concentration around us decreased, the entrance opened, the fog went away, and the sun came out—all in the space of about fifteen minutes. We decided those omens were good enough, so with Dave Logan steering, into the strait we went.
>
> Ocean Watch *entered the strait motoring along at 7 knots and exited the strait less than two hours later doing 14.5! The moving ice inside the channel made for some anxious moments*

Opposite page: What looked like a tower of ice in the distance was a refracted mirage, but the maze of pack ice in the foreground presented real challenges. *This page clockwise from top left:* From his perch in the spreaders, David Thoreson spied seals, ice floes, and piercing blue sculptures of ice.

for all but with good spotting help from the crew, Logan steered us around the large floes, avoided the rocks, and found the right track through the whole mess.

Making it through Bellot Strait and into Prince Regent Inlet is a huge accomplishment for us. Zenith Point, in the middle of Bellot Strait and situated on the northern tip of Boothia Peninsula, is the most northern point of continental North America. Ocean Watch and crew—with much help from the Around the Americas team—have now left that important milestone to starboard and behind us. All are okay and happy aboard Ocean Watch.

FARTHEST NORTH

We were out of the pack ice. But we weren't out of the woods. From Prince Regent Inlet, we continued north into Lancaster Sound, where we reached the northernmost point on our expedition Around the Americas: 73°53' N. The weather had turned, and we found ourselves bashing upwind in staunch easterlies. Icebergs now dotted the horizon. Luckily, they were big and visible, so we simply steered around them.

Then, shortly after the late dusk on August 28, we slipped into the corridor of water known as Navy Board Inlet on the northern shores of Baffin Island and were startled to see tall, craggy peaks; steeps freckled with snow; and before long, glaciers spilling from an ice field into the sea. After the low, flat Arctic landscape, it was like another planet.

At noon local time, under blue skies and with the distant glaciers and mountains of Bylot Island serving as a striking backdrop, *Ocean Watch*'s anchor rattled down off the tiny village of Pond Inlet as her crew put the finishing touches on their successful 2009 transit of the Northwest Passage. In so doing, *Ocean Watch* became the first American yacht ever to complete a west-to-east transit of the elusive northern waterway in a single season, and only the third U.S. boat in history to successfully negotiate the passage in an eastward direction.

The first American boat ever to tackle the Northwest Passage from west to east was legendary contemporary Arctic explorer and author John

Opposite page: En route to historic Gjoa Haven, Ocean Watch *rendezvoused with two British Royal Marines tackling the Northwest Passage in a 17-foot (5-m) open boat. Off Gjoa (top), ice experts aboard the Canadian icebreaker,* Sir Wilfrid Laurier *(above right), delivered surprising weather news.*

Bockstoce's 59-foot (18-m) motor-sailer, *Belvedere*, during a five-year span from 1983 to 1988. The second was *Arctic Wanderer*, a 59-foot (18-m) yacht skippered by Gary Ramos, from 2005 to 2008. The *Ocean Watch* team was honored to join the ranks of these fine sailors and crews. When all was said and done, all eleven vessels that sailed north of the Arctic Circle and into the Northwest Passage in 2009 completed the voyage—a record number. It was the third straight year in which every boat that had attempted the trip succeeded. As sailors, it was cause for celebration. But in the larger scheme, it was bittersweet. The reason everyone had made it was simple: the Arctic ice cap is receding at a record pace.

"The unprecedented 2007 shrinkage of polar ice cover to just 4.13 million square kilometers [1.75 million square miles]—nearly matched (in 2008) when only a 4.52-million-square-kilometer [1.6-million-square-mile] expanse of ice was left by mid-September—has led many forecasters to envision a virtually ice-free Arctic," wrote environmental reporter Randy Boswell shortly before our arrival in Pond Inlet. "Scientists believe the ongoing retreat is being driven by several factors, including rising global temperatures associated with human-induced climate change and the associated breakup and loss of thicker, multiyear ice that is being replaced only seasonally by a thin layer of winter ice that disappears quickly each summer."

In 2009, the negative trend continued: though it took longer for the leads to open up, ultimately, the Arctic suffered its third largest loss of sea ice ever, right behind the losses of 2007 and 2008. Indeed, satellite imagery revealed that during the last several years the polar ice cap had disappeared to a shocking degree. Australian scientist Tim Flannery addressed this topic in his book *The Weather Makers*.

"At its current rate of decline, little if any of the Arctic ice cap will be left by the end of the century," he noted, "and this will significantly change the Earth's 'albedo.' *Albedo* describes the mechanism through which solar energy is reflected back to space by white surfaces like the polar ice caps, an important factor in global climate control.

"One-third of the sun's rays falling on Earth is reflected back to space," he continued. "Ice, particularly at the Poles, is responsible for a lot of that albedo, for it reflects back into space up to 90 percent of the sunlight hitting it. Water, in contrast, is a poor reflector.

"When the sun is overhead, it reflects a mere 5 to 10 percent of light back to space, though, as you may have noticed while watching a sunset by the sea, the amount of light reflected off water increases as the sun approaches the horizon. Replacing Arctic ice with a dark ocean will result in a lot more of the sun's rays being absorbed at the Earth's surface and reradiated as heat, creating local warming, which, in a classic example of a positive feedback loop, will hasten the melting of the remaining continental ice."

Safely anchored in Pond Inlet, the Northwest Passage in our wake, on one hand we couldn't have been happier. On the other . . .

TO THE INUIT PEOPLE, CLIMATE CHANGE IS NOT A TOPIC FOR DEBATE. FOR DECADES THEY'VE WITNESSED RADICAL ALTERATIONS IN ICE, LAND, WATER, AND WILDLIFE.

In the Inuit towns above the Arctic Circle, the locals were always quick with a smile *(opposite page)* and have learned to make the most of the short northern summer *(above)*. **Top:** Educator Zeta Strickland attracted a youthful and eager crowd in Cambridge Bay. **Following pages:** Pond Inlet, on Baffin Island, marked the end of *Ocean Watch*'s successful Northwest Passage transit.

CHAPTER 5
INTO THE FRAY

On the first day of September 2009, three months after departing Seattle, *Ocean Watch* set forth from Pond Inlet for St. John's, Newfoundland, an 1,800 nautical-mile offshore passage down the coasts of Baffin Island and Labrador via three significant bodies of open ocean: Baffin Bay, the Davis Strait, and the Labrador Sea. For this leg of the journey—where we expected to encounter large icebergs that had broken free from the glaciers of Western Greenland—ice expert Harry Stern of the Applied Physics Lab at the University of Washington replaced the Pacific Science Center's educator Zeta Strickland on the crew roster. A newcomer to high-latitude voyaging, Stern had no idea what lay ahead of him.

For that matter, neither did the rest of us. Before setting out, as we'd done in each of the previous Nunavut villages we'd visited, we spent several hours topping up the diesel tanks with several hundred gallons of fuel, an arduous task that involved multiple runs ashore with the dinghy to fill our handful of 5-gallon (19-l) jugs from the local fuel truck. Like every other Inuit town in the far north, there was no dedicated fuel dock.

It was a warm, sunny afternoon, and the young man from the diesel depot mentioned to the captain that we were lucky to have such fine weather, as this was the first day of their short fall season, and they were expecting plunging temperatures and snow within a fortnight.

With that comment, the refueling operation took on a bit more urgency. Sure enough, by the time we'd drained the last jug of diesel into *Ocean Watch*'s tank, the skies had become overcast, and the calm waters began to ripple with a fresh breeze filling in from the east.

"Naturally, when we were ready to leave, the wind started blowing from the direction we wanted to go, the seas very quickly went from nothing to a steep 3- to 4-foot [1-m] chop, and our speed and comfort suffered accordingly," noted Skipper Schrader in his personal log.

> Sometime just before midnight, everything changed. The wind died, the sea became flat, and the fog rolled in to make a dark night even darker. Before long, radar echoes (targets) started popping up all over our Raymarine radar/chartplotter screen. Icebergs. Big ones. By dawn, we'd passed at least two dozen impressively large bergs close to our track.

> In the morning light, we got our first look at the impressive Baffin Island coastline. Dotted with hanging glaciers, high peaks, and entrances to multiple 50-mile-long (80-km-long) fjords, it would be a fantastic place to explore . . . just not now.

No, the timing wasn't right for exploration. For the first time in months, the compass needle was pointing in a new direction: south.

Above and opposite page: Once free of the pack ice in the enclosed channels of the Northwest Passage and into the open seas, *Ocean Watch* faced a new threat: icebergs calved from the glaciers of Western Greenland.

SURF'S UP

Twenty-four hours later, when Dave Logan stepped on deck for his morning watch, he counted thirty-three icebergs in our immediate vicinity. Some were large and daunting; others were small but stunning, as if created by the hand of a sculptor with an immaculate eye for form and geometry. Every so often, we'd encounter groups of bergs that resembled icy representations of Stonehenge. The multiple dots on the radar display made it appear as if it had contracted some electronic version of chickenpox. On we sailed.

By the third day, while fulmars (seabirds) danced upon the wave tops, there'd been a distinct change in the weather as the breeze shifted from the south into the northeast at a solid 20-plus knots. *Ocean Watch* reveled in the fresh conditions, broadreaching powerfully at speeds that reached as high as 10 knots.

"We're 44 tons of surfing fury," said Logan. But as far as the wind and seas were concerned, we hadn't seen anything yet.

Meanwhile, on board, there was only one fly in the ointment, but it left native Midwesterners Schrader and Thoreson—the former from Nebraska; the latter, Iowa—mightily annoyed. Though they searched our deep freezer time and again, we'd completely run out of . . . butter.

On September 4, we exited the Arctic Circle, which circles the high northern waters at a latitude of 66°33′ N. (Technically, this marked the official close of our Northwest Passage, the precise definition of which is a journey over the top of North America from the Arctic Circle to the Arctic Circle, either from the Atlantic to the Pacific or vice versa.) Two days later, in 20- to 30-knot westerlies some 200 nautical miles off the coast of Labrador, we recorded another milestone, as we passed the halfway point of the voyage to St. John's.

This highlight, underscored by the wispy and ethereal northern lights that had become a regular midnight attraction, came with some interesting news via the website for Environment Canada, the forecasting arm of the Canadian Weather Service: "Gale Warning in Effect." The Canadian meteorologists are very good, and once again, they were absolutely correct. Shortly thereafter, things became, as seasoned offshore sailors like to say, "sporty."

At first the breeze swung into the south and strengthened. It continued to build. Then it radically shifted from southwest to northwest and freshened still. The confluence of the old and new wave trains was shocking. When Logan and I came on watch at three in the morning, David Thoreson greeted us thusly: "I have some good news and some bad news. The good part is, it's starting to get light. The bad is, you can see what's going on."

Once the staunch northwesterly winds had filled in with a vengeance, they showed no sign of abating. *Ocean Watch* handled most

of the waves with grace and aplomb, letting them slide beneath her like a kid jumping rope. Most of the big rollers roared harmlessly by, though their backsides—what surfers call double overheads—were more than a little intimidating as they passed. The noise and motion were extreme and kept the crew busy with constant sail changes: tucking another reef in the main, swapping the forward jib for a tiny scrap of canvas called a storm staysail. But sailors can tell when a boat is balanced, safe, and in perfect trim, and for the most part, *Ocean Watch* was all that and more.

But the "liquid Himalayas" continued to build and grow, and at one stage, in a 45-knot gust of wind, *Ocean Watch* flew down the face of a monster—we estimated that the biggest waves were cresting at a good 30 feet (9 m)—at a best-ever speed of 17 knots. Off to leeward, we were shocked to discover what a fulmar looks like—flying backward.

On Labor Day, the skipper made the following entry in his personal log:

Gale conditions have been with us now for more than twenty-four hours. Our wind has clocked to the northwest, now blowing Beaufort Force 8 (fresh gale 34 to 40), average seas 12 feet (4 m), numerous sets well over 20 feet (6 m). Some seas are steep and breaking, others just spectacularly large.

We're currently broad reaching, taking wind and seas on the starboard aft quarter—at least that's what we're trying to do. Sometimes we get a little too broadside to the seas and lots of

Opposite page: In the Labrador Sea, *Ocean Watch* came up against a seventy-two-hour gale. **Top:** Winds in excess of 40 knots kept the crew scrambling to reduce sail in the rising weather. **Above:** Over time, the roiled seas crested to waves of 20 feet (6 m) and higher.

water comes aboard. Down below, Ocean Watch *is warm and dry; on deck and in the cockpit she is wet, even with our great side curtains.*

The Raymarine autopilot does an excellent job of steering in these very difficult conditions. Our average boat speed for the past few hours has been well over 8 knots. Sustained speeds of 12 to 14 aren't unusual. We're now rocketing under our storm staysail and deeply reefed main and running hard in front of some formidable mountains of water.

Forecast says we'll have this for a couple more days. This is certainly a three-to-four-strings-on-your-hat day. Breakfast, lunch, and dinner will be some variation of crackers and cheese. I'm finding it very difficult to hang on to the navigation station seat and type at the same time. It's time to strap myself in the bunk for a nap.

Two days later, not much had changed. Fast sailing it was. Pleasant sailing it was not. "The good news," wrote the skipper, "is a week ago we were in beautiful Pond Inlet, which is now covered with the first snowfall of the season, and now we're just a few miles from 'balmy' St. John's. The Labrador Sea has been and continues to be an athletic experience."

LANDFALL

For long-distance voyagers, the best part of a passage is almost always the end, when the hazards of the open ocean have been addressed and the destination is at hand. It's called landfall, and it never, ever gets old.

On the morning of September 11, at 3 AM local time, off to starboard, lights, shadows, and headlands began to emerge as if by magic. It was the coast of Newfoundland, emerging from the night. Terra firma. After getting pasted by gale-force winds for the previous seventy-two hours, it couldn't have been prettier.

The solid bits of planet Earth always look better when you haven't seen them for a while, which had been the case for more than a week. The coast of Labrador, along which we'd supposedly been sailing for several days, had been no more than a rumor, a concept we never fully grasped. We'd heard it was beautiful, harsh, stark, and memorable. We never saw it. Instead, we'd been well offshore, dealing with high blue slabs of water—and not always with complete success. Skidding down the face of a 25-foot (8-m) wave sideways in a substantial, 64-foot (20-m) steel missile—as we had on more than one occasion—had been an extremely interesting experience. It was one we didn't hope to repeat.

At dawn, the weather had finally changed in our favor: high pressure had settled over the Canadian Maritimes, accompanied by welcome blue skies. The crystal-clear morning light put a sharp, hard edge on the broad, wide vista; it was the sort of tint and glow that defines the angles and shadows in ways that are hard to describe. It made the world look fresh and clean, scrubbed anew.

A trio of headlands was lined up in a row, three solid Kirk Douglas–like chins of land speckled with patches of green. What a color. It had been so long since we'd seen it. Not only were the promontories and birds and fishing boats and houses—and look, a castle!—a treat to the senses, but so too were the earthy aromas, strong and pungent.

AFTER A TEN-DAY
OFFSHORE PASSAGE
DODGING GALES
AND ICEBERGS, THE
HAVEN OF ST. JOHN'S
WAS LIKE AN OASIS
IN A DESERT.

Big bullets of breeze came pulsing off the points, flecking the water with whitecaps. At the helm, Logan pointed the boat into the breeze, setting a new course, straight for the coast, toward a lighthouse perched on a rock. It served as the marker to a cleft in the cliffs, dark and severe, the slimmest of gaps.

We motored into the narrow cut, holding our collective breath, and then, suddenly, we found ourselves winding through the amazing, open harbor of St. John's. Logan swung the bow into the wind. Down came the mainsail. Out came the fenders and dock lines.

Cars. Skyscrapers. For heaven's sake, after weeks and weeks: A city. People strolling down a sidewalk. Logan feathered *Ocean Watch* alongside a pier. Moments later: Tied up. Secure. Stopped. Parked. Over.

We looked at each other. Took deep breaths. Laughed out loud.

After all the waves and wind and drama and tension of the last ten days, after the final 1,800 nautical miles of this 6,000-nautical-mile odyssey from distant Seattle across a storm-tossed sea, after the icebergs and the cold and the barren, wild, unforgettable Arctic—landfall.

Newfoundland. Landfall.

After ten days at sea, the lighthouse at the entrance to the harbor of St. John's, Newfoundland *(above)*, was a welcome sight, as was the appropriately named "Narrows" cut to the enclosed waters *(top)*. *Opposite page:* Once inside, the bustle along the colorful city front pleasantly assaulted our senses.

SCIENCE ABOARD OCEAN WATCH

In collaboration with the Pacific Science Center, the expedition's cosponsor, the Applied Physics Lab at the University of Washington, was one of a half-dozen scientific institutions and organizations that developed the *Ocean Watch* science program. Other expedition partners included the Joint Institute for the Study of the Atmosphere and Ocean (JISAO), MIT Sea Grant, the National Weather Service, the National Oceanic and Atmospheric Administration (NOAA), and NASA. Before leaving Seattle, the crew received instructions and tutorials on several projects for which they collected data, information, and samples during the course of the voyage. Once the journey was under way, several scientists joined the team for various legs of it.

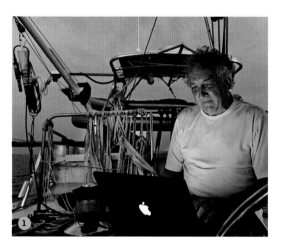

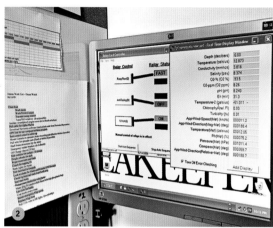

1) Oceanographer Michael Reynolds was the first scientist to join the crew, and he completed much of the voyage on subsequent legs. 2) The SeaKeeper underwater sampling system pumped seawater aboard to measure water temperature, sea salinity, pH levels, and dissolved oxygen concentrations. A conductivity-temperature-depth (CTD) model was lowered into the ocean twice daily to a depth of 131 feet (40 m) to "profile" temperatures and salinity in the upper water column. 3–4) In addition, a pH sensor provided a picture of the upper ocean acidity. 5) In the Northwest Passage, *Ocean Watch* deployed three Arctic Sea weather buoys for ice scientist Ignatius Rigor of the Applied Physics Lab. 6) The skipper examines Michael Reynolds's "climate package"—a 25-pound (11-kg) array of instruments mounted on the boat's masthead that included devices to record wind, temperature, relative humidity, and barometric pressure. Combined with accurate sea-surface temperature information, the goals were to measure the total heat energy going into the ocean, to get a better grasp on how solar radiation is affected by clouds and aerosols, and to gain greater insight into the dynamics of melting polar ice caps.

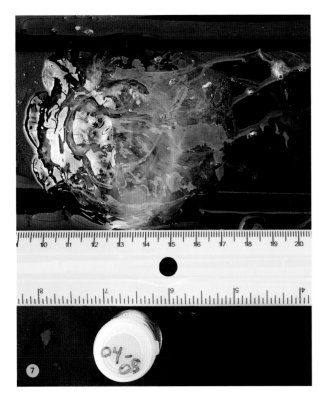

7–9) Jellyfish have been called the "canary in the coal mine" in ocean research because their health is an important indicator of the overall health of the seas. The mission of *Ocean Watch*'s "jellyfish survey" was to take measurements, photographs, and samples of jellyfish we encountered and to track and record positions of jellyfish colonies during the course of our travels. 10) A custom-installed camera called the Ladybug, affixed to a sliding boom on the aft antenna arch, was actually composed of six separate cameras in a single housing. The Ladybug recorded tens of thousands of individual images daily.

11) The camera then stitched the images together through a software program that afforded a 360-degree view of the horizon, the purpose of which was to monitor sea states and sea life atop the waters through which we sailed. 12) For a National Weather Service forecasting program, *Ocean Watch* filed real-time observations of wind direction, temperature, clouds, and visibility. 13) Our "sun photometer" measured the effect of atmospheric aerosols on solar energy reaching Earth's surface.

A VANISHING WAY OF LIFE

On the shores of the small Inuit village of Tuktoyaktuk, or "Tuk," hunter and fisherman Wayne Thrasher continues to practice the subsistence traditions passed down through the generations. But with a changing environment and the introduction to the Arctic of modern "conveniences" such as refrigeration and processed foods—obesity and diabetes have become serious issues in communities like Tuk in recent years—fewer and fewer Inuit are clinging to time-honored customs.

During a twelve-day period in the late summer of 2009, Wayne caught and smoked more than three hundred whitefish (or *bipsi*) and cleaned out a Beluga whale. His fish camp on the shores of Tuk *(opposite page, top)* is a model of efficiency: He catches the fish with gill nets in the nearby waters, then cleans and fillets them *(opposite page, bottom)* before they're smoked in the adjacent smokehouse. Afterward, he hangs the fish on the neat, tidy rows of drying racks erected on the site *(above)*.

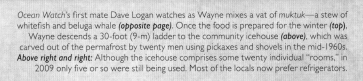

Ocean Watch's first mate Dave Logan watches as Wayne mixes a vat of *muktuk*—a stew of whitefish and beluga whale *(opposite page)*. Once the food is prepared for the winter *(top)*, Wayne descends a 30-foot (9-m) ladder to the community icehouse *(above)*, which was carved out of the permafrost by twenty men using pickaxes and shovels in the mid-1960s. *Above right and right:* Although the icehouse comprises some twenty individual "rooms," in 2009 only five or so were still being used. Most of the locals now prefer refrigerators.

PART 2

THE LONG SLOG SOUTH

CHAPTER 6
DOWN THE EASTERN SEABOARD

I n the midst of his journey above the Arctic Circle, which he described eloquently in his entrancing book, *North to the Night*, voyager Alvah Simon wrote, "Canada is captivating, in no small part due to Canadians." Aboard *Ocean Watch*, on an eventful trip through the Canadian Maritimes, we discovered the simple truth in Simon's prophetic observation.

In the friendly city of St. John's, Newfoundland, our hosts for the layover, the faculty and staff of the remarkable Fisheries and Marine Institute of Memorial University, treated us royally. Our visit to the campus included meetings with scientists and educators, a tour of the world's largest "ice tank" and the more conventional 656-foot (200-m) tow tank employed by the school's naval architecture students, and even a wild "ride" off the coast of Labrador via the institute's state-of-the-art ship simulator—almost as harrowing as the one we'd actually experienced aboard *Ocean Watch*.

Not long after, in Halifax, Nova Scotia, a capacity crowd for our presentation at the excellent Maritime Museum of the Atlantic showed us yet another humbling welcome. Then, Skipper Mark Schrader and onboard educator Zeta Strickland visited two sixth-grade classes at the Sir Charles Tupper School, and the next day, the kids came on a field trip to *Ocean Watch*.

The youngsters seemed to have a good time, but perhaps not as much fun as we sailors on board had.

So, yes, we couldn't get enough of the Canadian people.

But the Canadian weather was quite another story.

We left St. John's for the 510-nautical-mile trip to Halifax a day after Newfoundland was racked with a southerly gale packing wind gusts well in excess of 50 knots.

The morning of our departure, as soon as we'd left the protection of the inner harbor, we motored directly into a brisk southwesterly breeze accompanied by rather mountainous leftover seas from the previous day's storm. It was almost like a simulation of the simulator: calm one moment, crazy the next. The rest of the trip presented more lowlights than high ones.

The subsequent stop in Halifax was relaxing, but after several days it was again time to pay the piper, who served up the same woeful tune. The 360-nautical-mile trip southward featured a pair of gales, one from the south and the other from the north. They were bookends of misery. The three-day sail felt like a three-week ordeal.

But then, early on the third day at sea, from some 40 nautical miles out, the loom of a big city hove into view. Boston. The U.S. of A. For the crew of *Ocean Watch*, it looked like Oz. In many ways, it was.

As *Ocean Watch* traveled toward the equator, visits to Halifax, Nova Scotia *(above)*, and Boston, Massachusetts *(opposite)*, held memorable moments.

BEANTOWN TO THE BIG APPLE

On a gorgeous fall morning in late September, with the fresh light of the rising sun reflected off the high-rises lining the waterfront, *Ocean Watch* wound her way into Boston Harbor and sidled alongside the dock at Rowes Wharf in the hub of downtown Boston. We were just shy of four months into our journey, and the ship's log stated that we'd sailed precisely 8,492 nautical miles since leaving Seattle. It seemed like a lot until we realized we still had 19,000 more to go.

The next fortnight was a whirlwind. After several days in Boston, *Ocean Watch* set sail for the 100-nautical-mile overnight dash to historic Newport, Rhode Island. Luckily, for both nerves and schedules—we were now working backward from our rendezvous with Cape Horn off the far reaches of South America, which we needed to reach by late January at the height of the Southern Hemisphere summer—it was a mostly uneventful run with the highlight being the wee-hours ramble through the colorfully lit Cape Cod Canal on a beautiful September eve.

Following forty-eight frantic hours in Newport, catching up with old sailing mates and telling our story to a packed room at the New York Yacht Club's "station" in a mansion called Harbor Court, *Ocean Watch* was again under way—this time bound for New York City by way of the inside route down Long Island Sound.

A warm front was moving in, and showers were forecast, but we had only a couple of brief squalls and sailed under a bright, full moon for much of the night. Lucky. By sheer coincidence, we hit The Race, the notorious entrance to the sound, on the last of a fair tide that shot us through at 10 knots. The breeze never topped 20 knots and blew steadily out of the south-southeast. The miles passed quickly.

Arriving in New York by sea is always a singular experience, but for those of us who'd been making the trip for decades, the absence of the iconic Twin Towers of the World Trade Center on Manhattan's skyline remained difficult to reconcile.

Nonetheless, taking in the East River, the Chrysler Building, the United Nations building, the famous bridges, the Statue of Liberty, Ellis Island, and finally, the Hudson River—all from the deck of our increasingly well-traveled steel cutter—was still one amazing ride. At noon on October 3, we tied up at the Intrepid Sea-Air-Space Museum in the heart of the Big Apple.

In what was becoming a recurring theme, the best part of the New York call was relating our adventures to local students. Captain Schrader and David Thoreson met hundreds of inner-city kids through the city's Power of One program, passing along stories about ocean conservation, the waters that surround their metropolis, and the pure magic that can come from following dreams. As always in these encounters, the *Ocean Watch* crew reaped the greatest rewards.

The pleasant days in Manhattan passed quickly. An unexpected test waited just over the horizon.

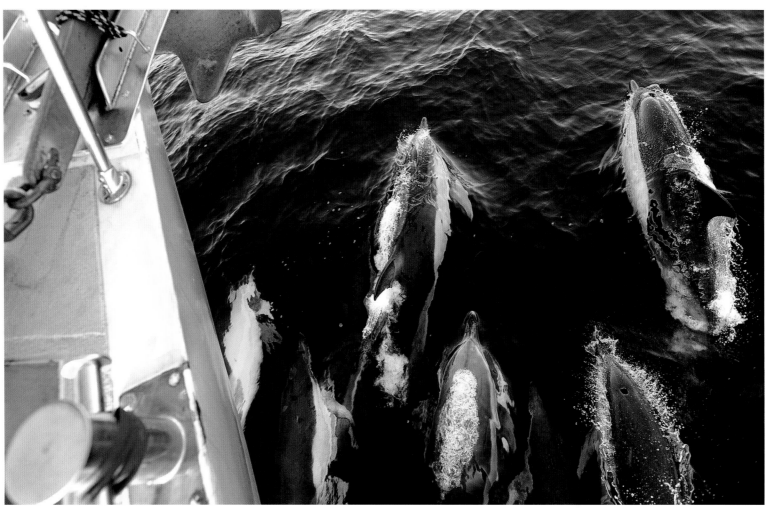

Above: Atlantic white-sided dolphins kept us company on the sail down the coast. *Opposite page:* In New York City, the Statue of Liberty and the crowds at the Intrepid Museum *(top right)* were welcome sights. Though we'd endured rough conditions to get to the Big Apple *(center right)*, Skipper Schrader was pleased to arrive *(bottom right)*.

GULF CREAMED

In 1768, the deputy postmaster of the British American colonies—a chap named Benjamin Franklin—became fascinated by North Atlantic ocean currents and circulation because merchant ships traveling from the United Kingdom to the East Coast cities of Newport and New York were completing the passage weeks faster than the mail packets sailing the identical route. Franklin's question couldn't have been simpler: Why?

Franklin sought the counsel of his cousin, Timothy Folger, a Nantucket whaler, who explained that the merchant skippers crossed a powerful eastward flowing current—identifiable by noticeable changes in temperature and color—while the packet captains bashed their way directly into it, significantly slowing their progress. (As a contemporary example, they were walking up a down escalator.) Franklin pursued his research with other ships' captains and realized the powerful current originated in the Gulf of Mexico near the tip of Florida and flowed north up the East Coast of North America and Newfoundland before turning east across the Atlantic. Franklin published his first chart of this independent "river in the sea" in 1770. He called it the "Gulf Stream."

For the next 600-nautical-mile leg of the voyage, from New York to Charleston, South Carolina, *Ocean Watch*'s crew would have to not only confront the Gulf Stream, but also negotiate the so-called Graveyard of the Atlantic—Cape Hatteras, North Carolina—where the watery contour of the continental shelf recedes rapidly from deep to shallow. Many a ship had come to grief off the cape's shoal shores.

When we left New York late on the afternoon of October 9 and sailed under the Verrazano-Narrows Bridge into the open Atlantic, the forecast was complicated. A pair of fronts was moving across the country with dispatch. But the first twelve to fourteen hours of the trip were almost laconic, as we sidled down the coast of New Jersey through placid seas, making an easy 7 to 8 knots while motor sailing with a staysail and reefed main. Then, shortly after daybreak, the easy southwest wind built quickly to about 20 knots with gusts to about 25. The seas began to surge. We took in a second reef and held on with both fists.

The good news was that the strong headwinds forced us well offshore, which meant well clear of Cape Hatteras, and into the Sargasso Sea, the stunningly clear waters located in the crook of the Gulf Stream gyre that are so named for the golden seaweed that contrasts vividly against the blue ocean. As we spied the first few patches, we realized the current itself was close at hand. And that's when all hell broke loose.

The general idea at the outset had been to aim for a waypoint, or set of latitude and longitude coordinates, well away from Hatteras and then catch the ensuing northwest breeze into Charleston once the cold front passed. That plan did not work.

Thirty-six hours into the trip, we sailed into the Gulf Stream and directly into the teeth of 30 to 40 knots of southwest breeze. As *Ocean Watch* crashed and splashed its way into the opposing seaway, running at a good 2 to 3 knots in concert with the current, the noise, motion, and violence of the storm was just this side of overwhelming. Swept eastward by the current, we soon found ourselves some 170 nautical miles offshore, sailing *away* from Charleston. Oh dear.

Opposite page, top: Scientist Michael Reynolds was also a whiz in the galley. *Opposite page, bottom:* In South Carolina, a scientist at the Hollings Marine Laboratory explained how the metabolic activity of pathogens causes coral bleaching, a serious threat to undersea reef ecosystems worldwide. *Above: Ocean Watch* enters the harbor in South Carolina.

At least it was warm; water temperatures registered over 80° F (27° C). But even that was a double-edged sword: With *Ocean Watch* continuously swept from bow to stern by boarding waves, we had to keep all hatches and ports shut, and the interior soon felt like a sauna, topping out at over 90° F (32° C). Above and belowdecks, there was little relief.

All that said, the Gulf Stream itself, basking in the fair-weather gale, was incredibly picturesque, featuring dramatic clouds at sunrise, piercing rays of sunlight radiating off the waves, and schools of porpoises cavorting in the bow wave. We tried to keep reminding ourselves that not many people witness the Gulf Stream in all its glorious fury.

Of course, like all storms, this one eventually passed, and the second half of the trip was fast and easy. Six long days after leaving New York, we slipped inside the jetties marking the entrance to Charleston Harbor, passed Fort Sumter where the Civil War basically began in 1861, and found ourselves in yet another famous port that had played a major role in our nation's history.

MIAMI: NICE AND VICE

In both Charleston and Miami, the final stop on our route down the Eastern Seaboard, we had the chance to visit world-class scientific laboratories and research centers: the Hollings Marine Laboratory (HML) on the South Carolina shores of James Island, and the University of Miami's Rosenstiel School of Marine and Atmospheric Science, which hosted our layover in Florida.

The mission of the HML is "to provide science and biotechnology applications to sustain, protect, and restore coastal ecosystems, with an emphasis on links between the environment and the health of marine organisms and humans." The Rosenstiel School, meanwhile,

Above: In Miami, we were greeted by the fireboats from the Miami Fire Department, but the condition of the inner harbor wasn't pretty *(top)*. *Center:* Against the Miami skyline, *Ocean Watch* docks. *Opposite page:* Shake-A-Leg Miami's Harry Horgan inspired us with his commitment to education and conservation.

was founded in the mid-1940s and includes a 65-acre (26-ha) marine research and education park on Biscayne Bay. It has evolved into one of the world's leading oceanographic and atmospheric research institutions. At both institutions, we enjoyed touring the facilities and learning about specific research studies currently under way. As the voyage continued, our own onboard oceanographer, Michael Reynolds, expanded on what we'd learned on an almost daily basis.

Like the trip between St. John's and Halifax, the 400-nautical-mile passage from South Carolina to southern Florida was sailed in brisk winds, but this time, at last, they were coming from the right direction. Flirting with the boundaries of the opposing current of the Gulf Stream, we hit a few bumpy patches at the outset. But for the most part, *Ocean Watch* barreled down the coast before a fine north wind, and the crew enjoyed some of the fastest sailing since the Labrador Sea.

As we sailed into Miami from the blue Atlantic via the long waterway known as Government Cut, a pair of fireboats from the Miami Fire Department sent towering arcs of spray into the sky. We doused the mainsail and motored into our slip at Bicentennial Park, directly adjacent to the American Airlines Arena.

"We haven't seen that sort of welcome since the *Queen Mary* sailed into town," said one longtime Miami resident.

A couple of days later, the crew ventured to the outstanding facilities at Shake-A-Leg Miami for a pair of student outreach presentations to Miami-area students. Harry and Susie Horgan and Barth Green launched the organization to provide sailing, outdoor, and educational programs to physically challenged individuals, and it had expanded to include the greater Miami community at large. It had become Harry Horgan's lifework after he became a paraplegic in a car

THE BIRD FLOATING ATOP A SMALL SEA OF GUNK AND GARBAGE WOULD BE A RECURRING IMAGE AS OCEAN WATCH SET SAIL FOR SOUTH AMERICA.

accident many years ago. The Horgans are longtime friends and special people, and our time at Shake-A-Leg Miami was one of our best days since leaving Seattle. So our last stop on the East Coast was pleasant indeed, right up to the end. For as we sailed out of Miami in late October to resume our voyage, Thoreson took a photograph that would become etched in our memories—a bird floating on a Styrofoam life preserver in a small sea of gunk and plastic, undulating with the waves.

We were thinking "Miami vice," but, alas, it would be a recurring image in the many miles and months ahead.

CHAPTER 7

CROSSING THE LINE

Shortly before leaving Miami for the 900-nautical-mile passage through the Bahamas and then offshore to San Juan, Puerto Rico, Skipper Schrader said, "Miami is the gateway to the second part of our trip. The North is behind us. Now we're truly headed south."

The immediate itinerary seemed fairly straightforward. After a layover in Puerto Rico, we intended to set a course southward and cross the line that demarcates the Northern and Southern Hemispheres—the equator—and then continue more or less straight on to the Brazilian megalopolis of Rio de Janeiro.

That was the theory. But we'd soon discover that the best-laid plans can go awry.

On October 26, now with just over 10,000 nautical miles under the keel, *Ocean Watch* set sail for San Juan. Sailors often say the best way to get to the Caribbean from the U.S. East Coast is to sail due east "until the butter melts" at around 65° W latitude and then turn hard to starboard, thus ensuring the best sailing slant on the steady easterly trade winds.

Like the Gulf Stream, the trades are a powerful force of nature that blow steadily out of the east between the low-pressure Intertropical Convergence Zone (ITCZ) straddling the equator and the high-pressure belts about 30 degrees north and south of it. We reckoned the easterlies would be a handful on the initial leg to San Juan.

However, in Miami, we ran into a longtime sailing mate, John Kretschmer, a professional sailor and author who'd made the trip countless times, and he advised us to eschew the conventional routing wisdom and sail the rhumb line—the straight, shortest-distance-between-two-points option—after exiting the Bahamas and gaining the open Atlantic.

Soon after we slipped past the Bahamian isles on a breezy, bumpy night, the trades vanished completely, and we followed Kretschmer's advice and enjoyed an easy passage to Puerto Rico.

The best part of the trip was the night watch. Far from the loom of city lights, each evening we were treated to a spectacular light show of countless falling stars courtesy of the annual Orionids meteor shower, which occurs every October.

And then, halfway through the voyage, *Ocean Watch* crossed the Tropic of Cancer (at latitude 23°26' N, it's the position where the sun is directly overhead on the summer solstice) to officially enter the tropical portion of the voyage south.

On our final day in the open sea, a thick, gray layer of cloud and mist negated the glorious daily sunrise that had been a constant of the passage. The wind continued to rise, and the seaway became lumpy and dramatic. As we closed in on San Juan, the rolling waves crashed severely

Above: The crashing surf off the entrance to San Juan Harbor was an awesome sight, as were the squalls and general weather patterns in the doldrums as we neared the equator *(opposite page).*

84 ONE ISLAND, ONE OCEAN

Above (clockwise from bottom left): A local "entrepreneur" peddled his wares off St. Lucia, where, later, the crew got their first look at tropical skylines. We enjoyed both fast sailing and shoreside forays while transiting the Caribbean. *Opposite page:* Nightlight shows became a feature on the passage south.

against the rocky shore. We kept a sharp eye out for the sea buoy marking the channel leading into the harbor. Suddenly, there it was.

First mate Logan drove *Ocean Watch* down the well-marked corridor and into the inner harbor between sets of wild breakers to the east and the west. When the breeze and seas lay down, we dropped the mainsail, found our berth, secured our dock lines, and took teetering and unsure steps ashore. With the sun ascending overhead, the heat was suddenly searing. It was like walking on the sun.

Our host for the visit was the Department of Marine Sciences at the University of Puerto Rico, so, at the beginning of the week, a group of students and faculty, including director Nilda Aponte, visited *Ocean Watch*. A couple of days later we drove out of the city, bound for the school's laboratory, facilities, and docks on the 22-acre (9-ha) island of Magueyes, off the southwestern coastal town of Parguera.

There, under the direction of divemaster Milton Carlo, we donned scuba tanks and embarked on a drift dive on a site called Media Luna (Half Moon) Reef. Carlo explained to us that in 2005 almost 70 percent of the coral in much of the Caribbean was lost after a bleaching event that caused catastrophic damage over widespread areas. The exact cause remains unknown.

"It's very sad," he said, "to dive and see places where coral that was alive and beautiful existed not so long ago."

Though it was unsettling to see so much dead and blanched coral, in the latter stages of the dive we came upon a beautifully lit coral garden. The color and variety of the fan-like coral was exceptional.

"Those are the gorgonian corals," said Carlo. "Many scientists think they're the future of coral because the constant movement of the water washes away the sediments and algae."

On November 8, we were under way early on what was originally slated to be the longest single leg of the entire expedition—a nonstop, 3,500-nautical-mile passage to Rio.

The skipper had budgeted twenty-four days for *Ocean Watch* to make the trip. It didn't take long to realize that the notion of landing in Rio in just over three weeks' time wasn't only whimsical and optimistic; it bordered on lunacy.

UNPLANNED DETOURS

With Jen Price and Rick Fleischman aboard—seasoned Alaskan charter-boat operators and the skipper's friends—after setting sail from San Juan, we were all looking forward to some great sailing. What awaited us was something altogether different.

As we slipped south in light air through the maze of islands dotting the Caribbean Sea, we couldn't resist an overnight "pit stop in paradise" on the lush island of St. Lucia. Though it was a brief respite and we were quickly under way again, it wouldn't be the last of our unplanned detours.

Only in retrospect did it seem fitting that on Friday, November 13, we sailed out of the turquoise Caribbean and back into the deep blue Atlantic. Almost immediately, as if someone had flipped a switch, the easterly trade winds filled in—from the direction in which we were headed.

It didn't take long before Skipper Schrader made an executive decision regarding our route: rather than push on directly for Rio, we would aim for Fernando de Noronha, a Brazilian archipelago about 2,000 nautical miles away. But soon *Ocean Watch* was bucking into a nasty, 2-to-3-knot opposing current, further impeding our progress. At times our speed was a mere 3 to 4 knots.

Furthermore, because we were using so much fuel to batter our way upwind and up current—with a range under a combination of engine and sail of about 1,000 nautical miles—it soon became apparent that if we had any hope of rounding Cape Horn in January, we couldn't afford the luxury of an extended, open-ended voyage to Fernando de Noronha.

In other words, given our schedule and circumstances, we'd need to make a second, more urgent unplanned stop to top off the diesel tanks. Scanning the charts, there were few options. The closest, most direct alternative was the city of Cayenne, on the coast of French Guiana. In fact, we were aiming directly for it.

As we approached Cayenne on the afternoon of November 19, the color of the water changed from green, to greenish brown, to light brown, to a color that could be called liquid Fudgsicle, a thick, murky, almost chocolate-like substance made all the more bizarre by the wind and current stirring its flow. The coursing waterway leading into Cayenne bears a lyrical name—the Fleuve Mahury—but Dave Logan, at the helm, had a different handle, one that quite accurately described the scene we were witnessing.

"It looks like the river where cappuccino comes from," he said. What we were actually gazing at was the murky outflow of the Amazon River to the south.

Once the anchor was set in the ripping tidal flow at the head of the Fleuve Mahury, we stopped for a moment to take in our surroundings. Gazing at the jungle lining the canal, we had our first hard look at South America.

The only unsettling problem was, once we actually stepped ashore, it appeared that we'd landed in France.

Thirty miles (48 km) northwest of Cayenne, the European Space Agency's Spaceport is located in Kourou, French Guiana. The French, of course, are the driving force behind the facility, and they've invested countless euros, which explains the country's decidedly French flavor (as well as the three daily flights to and from Paris). Nothing happened quickly or easily in Cayenne, including our refueling operation, but after several days we managed to take on 300 gallons (1,136 l) of diesel fuel and resume our travels.

Figuratively speaking, it was like stepping back into the ring of a prizefight.

NORTH TO SOUTH

The world's complex system of ocean currents and countercurrents include, among others, the North and South Equatorial Currents; the Equatorial Countercurrent; the Agulhas Current, off South Africa; the Southern Ocean Current; and in the North Atlantic, the Gulf Stream, which gave us a rude spanking on the voyage from New York to Charleston. But for the moment, the notorious, northerly setting Brazilian Current had our full, undivided attention.

At times, *Ocean Watch* plowed through the boisterous seas making 7 to 8 knots through the water, but again, because of the relentless set of the current, only achieved 3 to 4 knots in terms of genuine progress towards our goal. To exacerbate the situation, we had sailed into the ITCZ, better known to sailors as the doldrums, where we encountered wildly fluctuating weather.

One instant we'd be scrambling to reef sail in a localized 40-knot squall. Fifteen minutes later, we'd be atop a calm, dark, windless sea, wallowing in the leftover swell.

Plus, it was hot, above decks and below. Still, on November 26, we fired up the oven and prepared a Thanksgiving turkey dinner with all the fixings. As we finished, we were wiping sweat from our brows.

A couple of days later, we neared the equator at last. Those of us in the crew who had not previously crossed it by sea—known in seaman's lore as "Pollywogs"—prepared for our initiation ceremony at the hands of those aboard who'd done so on past voyages—the "Sons of Neptune," or "Shellbacks." This rite of passage, known as "Crossing the Line," has been passed down through the generations aboard everything from naval ships to commercial vessels to cruising yachts. Originally, the tradition was created as a test for seasoned sailors to ensure their new shipmates were capable of handling long, rough times at sea. Happily, as we'd discover, the Shellbacks let us Pollywogs off without excessive drama or embarrassment, which is not always the case.

On November 28, at precisely 9:14 AM—as if watching numbers spin on a slot machine—the line of latitude on our chartplotter went from 00°00'.001 N to 00°00'.000 to 00°00'.001 S.

North became South. Fall became spring. We were no longer in the Northern Hemisphere. We were south.

"You are now in the antipodes," said oceanographer Michael Reynolds. "Anti. Pod. Upside down."

And so we were.

Opposite page: With *Ocean Watch* slamming upwind *(top)*, the "Pollywogs" prepared for their equator crossing *(bottom right)*. In the searing heat, we probably could have roasted our Thanksgiving dinner without the oven *(bottom left)*. *Above:* Belowdecks, everything from cooking to writing became a chore. *Following pages:* On deck, the views were worth it.

CHAPTER 8

BRAZIL'S BITTER BULGE

Shortly after crossing the equator, an email from Harry Stern, the ice scientist who'd sailed aboard *Ocean Watch* in the Northwest Passage, appeared in the boat's in-box. The fact-filled message confirmed a few matters we'd observed, several more that we'd been unaware of, and underscored the notion that our crossing of the equator had been more than symbolic.

For instance, Stern noted, Earth's surface is 29 percent land and 71 percent ocean, but most of the land is in the Northern Hemisphere and most of the ocean is in the Southern Hemisphere. The Northern Hemisphere is 55 percent ocean, while the Southern is 86 percent ocean. "*Ocean Watch*," Stern wrote, "has entered the water hemisphere."

Climates in the Southern Hemisphere (except Antarctica) tend to be slightly milder than those in the Northern Hemisphere because water heats up and cools down more slowly than land. "Oceans have a large thermal inertia," Stern reported.

We already noticed that the night we crossed the equator we'd said farewell to Polaris—the North Star—which is located directly above the North Pole, and which disappeared below the horizon once we'd entered the Southern Hemisphere.

For several days prior to the one on which *Ocean Watch* crossed the line, in the wee hours just before dawn, we'd begun to see the iconic Southern Cross—the constellation more or less above the South Pole.

It would remain the dominant feature in the night sky for the weeks and months ahead.

"You can also say good bye to 90 percent of humanity now," concluded Stern. "Only about 10 percent of the human population lives south of the equator." So we'd entered a new and wondrous world, ashore and at sea, now that we'd made our way to the southern portion of the planet. The only problem was, we weren't actually heading south; the compass was still pointing east.

Six days after leaving Cayenne, and some forty-eight hours after crossing the equator—tacking endlessly into fierce currents and going nowhere fast—we pulled into the bustling industrial port of Itaqui, adjacent to the coastal Brazilian city of São Luís, for another unscheduled visit to refill the fuel tanks. According to the trip log, we had "sailed" 1,200 nautical miles since leaving Cayenne, though the true point-to-point mileage accrued was just 720 nautical miles. South of the equator, our southing had come to a halt. To make our way around the endless northern coastline of Brazil, which bulged far into the Atlantic like an old boxer leading with his chin, we needed to keep rolling east.

We were learning, firsthand, that one doesn't really understand how vast Brazil is until sailing around it. Yet Brazil's sheer girth wasn't as much of an issue as those confounded northern currents coupled with the prevailing southeasterly winds; together, they presented a formidable obstacle.

Above and opposite page: The sailing prowess of the Brazilian fishermen in their simple crafts continually impressed us. *Following pages:* The coastal waters at the outflow of the Amazon River were rich in sediment.

THE SOUTHERN HEMISPHERE, OVER 80 PERCENT OF WHICH IS COMPOSED OF OCEAN, IS "THE WATER HEMISPHERE."

EASTWARD TO CABO CALCANHAR

The sad truth is, we had no one to blame but ourselves. Much later, we received a bit of tongue-in-cheek advice from a seasoned passage-making friend with the "proper" sailing instructions for a jaunt from the Caribbean to Rio: "Head directly for the Canary Islands. When you see them, turn right." In other words, use the trade winds to your advantage by sailing around and above the South Atlantic's high-pressure ridge. In essence, opting for what was in theory a shorter route, we'd decided to follow a direct rhumb line course from the islands to Cabo Calcanhar, the Brazilian cape at the tip of the country's extreme eastern bulge. And we paid the consequences.

In our defense, we'd heard from several extremely reliable sources that a southerly countercurrent coursing at up to 3 knots ran parallel to the well-known and established Brazilian Current that flows northward up the coast. That's what we went searching for. We never found it.

In São Luís, we bid farewell to our Alaskan friends, Rick Fleischman and Jen Price, who needed to fly home for family commitments. Or at least that's what they said.

Carrying forward, Skipper Schrader now had two choices for our next harbor-hopping port of call, the tactic to which we were now committed. The closest port was Fortaleza, a few hundred miles away but still west of Cabo Calcanhar. Natal was a good 600 nautical miles down the track, but it had a powerful allure: it was south of the outlying cape, and putting Calcanhar behind us had become an obsession.

For better or worse, our next stop would be Natal.

On December 1, we punched our way out through the long channel leading in and out of São Luís and back into the open Atlantic. Since we'd tried everything else, we decided to hug the shoreline and perhaps find some current relief inshore. Twenty-four hours later, it appeared that our strategy was paying off. Though we were still slamming into 20-knot easterlies, we were bucking only a knot or two of current, and sometimes less. Finally, on the 185th day of our travels, it seemed as if we were once again getting somewhere.

Still, three days later, sliding eastward along the fourth parallel, just south of 4° S, we slipped through a series of strange, top-heavy oil derricks that appeared to be standing on one spindly leg, defying the laws of physics and gravity. Moreover, for weeks the midday cabin temperature never dropped below 92° F (33° C). The stifling heat continued to affect everyone's mood and everyone's movement, or, more accurately, the almost complete lack thereof. In the north, the prevailing onboard buzz always seemed to be upbeat, the energy always positive. To this stage, in the south, lassitude had prevailed.

But the following day, on December 6, just before we figuratively went "around the bend," we did so literally, putting Cabo Calcanhar behind us. The previous night had felt endless. A series of blobs appeared on the radar, signifying small cells of rain and wind, little squalls. For hours and hours, our latitude never wavered as we headed east: 4°45' S. At midmorning, we took a tentative tack southward. By midafternoon, we were abeam of Calcanhar. By 4 PM local time, we'd crossed 5° S, and the next morning we were safely in Natal.

RIO DE JANIERO ROUTE

Atlantic Ocean

Ponta Santo Cristo

Cabo Calcanhar

BRAZIL

Toure

0   5
miles

Opposite page: Off the coast of Brazil, spindly oil rigs were ubiquitous *(top)*. Due to the headwinds and Brazilian current, our unscheduled stops included Cayenne, French Guiana *(center and bottom)*. *Above:* This is how our chartplotter looked as we neared Cabo Calcanhar.

Rio was still more than 1,000 nautical miles away, but that evening we celebrated, in equal measures of joy and relief.

CHANGES IN ATTITUDE

On the morning of December 8, we departed the concrete docks at Natal's yacht club, and motored back out of the mangrove-lined Rio Potengi, and returned to the south Atlantic Ocean. But at that juncture, not only did our heading change—just a tad east of south—so did our luck.

Precisely twenty-four hours later, the bright orange sun rose to the east right as the skyline of Recife hove into view to the west. *Ocean Watch* was sandwiched between the two, and the vantage point was illuminating. Recife is home to millions of Brazilians, many of whom live in the endless array of skyscrapers that line the waterfront. The glowing solar orb reflecting off the glass facades of the high-rises was fiery and brilliant.

But the glorious sunrise wasn't the day's only high point, as the skipper noted in his personal log for the day:

> *We've made special note of several milestones along the way over the past six and a half months, and early this morning at mile number 14,408—roughly halfway around the Americas—we recorded a big one. On July 8 in the middle of the Bering Strait, we sailed*

Top and above: Five weeks out of San Juan, the sight of Rio de Janeiro's *Christo Redentor* atop the Pico do Corcovado, as well as its local fishing fleet, were promising signs. *Opposite:* From our berth at Rio's Marina da Gloria, we enjoyed the sunshine and waterfront ambience.

through the westernmost point of the voyage. At Zenith Point, midway through Bellot Strait, on August 26, we rounded the northernmost point of the journey. And . . . this morning, we sailed through the easternmost point. It is particularly satisfying to have this eastern one behind us. It was a long slog up a high mountain in uncomfortable shoes. All points have had their unique challenges, as will the upcoming southern point at Cape Horn, but this one was sweet.

At the early-morning watch change, we were able to set all the working sails—main, jib, and staysail—and give the Lugger engine a rest. . . . It is one of those magic, flat-water, gentle-breeze, cloudless-sky days on the ocean. With 11 knots of breeze Ocean Watch is close reaching at a steady and very quiet 7 knots. We're doing a little better over the ground thanks to a half-knot current that is now flowing with us along the coast toward Rio de Janeiro and points south.

With a nod toward musician Jimmy Buffett, the changes in latitude did bring a change in our attitudes. Before long, the wind swung aft, and we were able to hoist our distinctive billowing white spinnaker, emblazoned with a logo of North and South America. It had been months since we'd enjoyed the proper conditions to fly it. And with the engine shut down for the first time in eons, the silence truly was golden.

A week after leaving Natal, on December 15, we sailed out of the windy southern Atlantic Ocean and into the beautiful and lush Bay of St. Lucy, at the mouth of the Rio de Janeiro—the "River of January."

Those of us who'd been there before recognized the familiar profile of the mountain called Sugarloaf, and the towering 2,300-foot (701-m) peak known as Pico do Corcovado, topped by the tall, striking statue of Jesus—*Christo Redentor* in Portuguese, or Christ the Redeemer—his arms open to the sea.

Entering the harbor, our eyes shifted from the prominent landmarks above to the rows of residential towers lining the beaches of Copacabana and Ipanema. Before long we'd wended our way behind a breakwater near the airport and secured a mooring at Marina da Gloria. For the next couple of days, this would be our home and base of operations.

We were thirty-seven days out of San Juan, a good two weeks behind our proposed itinerary for the trip. It seemed like two years.

CHAPTER 9
THE ROARING FORTIES

Despite the encouraging conclusion of our passage to Rio de Janeiro, we tied up in the teeming city with no small sense of trepidation. During the journey from Miami, we'd all read a feature story about Rio from a recent issue of *The New Yorker* magazine that described a crime-ridden place with an astronomical murder rate, a city governed in equal measure by corrupt cops and rampant gangs.

Our fears and worries proved unfounded. Maybe it was because we frequented the secure facilities of our berth at the Marina da Gloria or busy tourist spots like the strip along Copacabana Beach, or maybe Brazil was already getting its act together now that it's been awarded the 2016 Summer Olympics. Whatever the cause, the Rio we discovered was orderly, beautiful, inviting, and sensual—all qualities on which its reputation was originally built. For us, Rio de Janeiro was a pleasant surprise.

On December 18, after the quick 75-nautical-mile run from Rio, we made our final stop in Brazil at a resort town called Angra dos Reis, in the popular tourist and sailing region of bays, beaches, and islands known as Ilha Grande. In some aspects, Ilha Grande looked like the Pacific Northwest (think San Juan Islands or British Columbia); in others, like certain choice parts of southern Europe (think Italy or Croatia). It had taken three full weeks to negotiate Brazil's coastline, and under different circumstances—not only for Brazil's breathtaking beauty

but also because of its welcoming people—we could've lingered there for an entire season or two of relaxing cruising. But Punta del Este, Uruguay, was 900 nautical miles to the south, and we needed to keep moving.

Our luck held on the run to Punta, with brisk northerlies propelling *Ocean Watch* down the South American coastline under the clearest skies imaginable. We arrived in the affluent Uruguayan city on December 23 and were greeted warmly at the Yacht Club Punta del Este—where several of us had forged friendships on previous trips—just in time for the Christmas holidays. It's something we'll never forget.

Following Uruguayan custom—celebrating the holiday on Christmas Eve—we dined late at a terrific restaurant, where just before midnight, waiters passed around flutes of champagne, and everyone gathered outside on the tiled boardwalk ringing the harbor and watched dozens of impromptu fireworks displays across the city and along the beaches. Strangers clinked glasses, everyone wished everyone else a joyous yuletide, and we all felt very much part of something special.

The only problem was a minor one: the weather was unseasonably cold and foggy. And the strange trend continued on our overnight run to Mar del Plata, Argentina. It started two days after Christmas in brilliant sunshine. The wind went aft and we enjoyed some fine sailing through the afternoon. The breeze picked up at night and kept moving aft to the

Above: A classic cigar-shaped cold front barreled off the coast of South America. *Opposite page:* Swirling and alive as it rendezvoused with *Ocean Watch*, the cloud formation was a fitting greeting to the notorious roaring forties.

north, then abruptly shifted forward, into the south. The resulting seas were awful, with standing water in some spots that made for a bucking-bronco experience. Stars came out and went away. The whitecaps on the dark water appeared absolutely electric, almost as if a powerful beam of light illuminated them from beneath the sea. Dawn was dark, and the wind continued to rise. When it hit 35 knots, we struck all sails and motored into Mar del Plata in the late afternoon, licking our wounds.

"That was like à la carte sailing," said Roxanne Nanninga of Seattle's Pacific Science Center; she was not only our new onboard educator but also a rookie sailor who fared remarkably well in dire conditions during her first foray on *Ocean Watch*. What she meant, we surmised, was that there'd been a little bit of everything weather-wise. She was right.

We spent several days in Mar del Plata, taking in New Year's Eve at a wild bash at the local yacht club. Once the weather cleared, we found ourselves stunned by the tens of thousands of bathers and sun worshippers who descended on the resort city's series of beaches nestled among the rocky cliffs and headlands. "These crowds," said Skipper Schrader, gazing at the incredible mass of humanity, "are loving the ocean to death."

Perhaps, but the sunny weather meant we had no chance to linger. Now into January, we needed to continue our progress to Cape Horn.

THE FANTASTIC FORTIES

Ocean Watch was at the very doorstep of the so-called roaring forties and screaming fifties: the high latitudes of the Southern Hemisphere. Both bands of ocean, each some 600 nautical miles wide—the former between 40° and 50° S, the latter from 50° to 60° S (with the Horn, at 56° S, almost smack-dab in the center)—earned their sobriquets from ancient mariners who'd been tested in those distant waters.

The powerful westerly winds that scream and roar owed their existence to the geographical fact that there are few major landmasses at the bottom of the planet, permitting tightly wound fronts of low pressure to gather force and carry onward largely unimpeded, spinning

DAVID THORESON GRINNED MANIACALLY. "WELCOME TO THE ROARING FORTIES," HE QUIPPED.

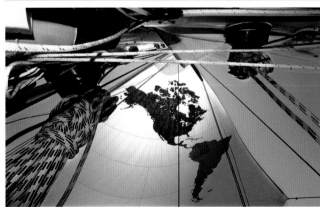

Opposite page, top and bottom: We furled our mainsail upon our final approach to the Uruguayan coastal city of Punta del Este. *This page, clockwise from top:* After the initial roaring forties gale, we enjoyed some rollicking sailing under our big asymmetric spinnaker and, later, a poled-out headsail.

the seas into frothy mayhem and leaving the hapless sailors tossed upon them holding on for dear life.

As the tall ship merchant seaman from the Great Age of Sail used to say: "Beyond 40° South there is no law. Beyond 50° there is no God."

Ironically, when we left Mar del Plata bound for the Falkland Islands on January 5, for the first few hours we enjoyed some delightful sailing, with bright sunshine and a following breeze. But we were well aware that it wouldn't last. We'd been tracking a low that was born in the Andes Mountains and came funneling out of the River Plate, as do so many Southern Ocean storms. We realized that it would only be a matter of time before we rendezvoused, most likely in unpleasant circumstances.

Sure enough, just before dusk, only a few miles north of the fabled fortieth parallel, the sky to the west darkened, and we took the opportunity in the fading daylight to shorten our mainsail down to the second reef. We didn't have to wait long before the dramatic, clearly defined, cigar-shaped cold front was upon us. It was a dozen shades of gray, swirling and alive, beautiful yet imposing, scary yet awesome. At first it seemed to suck every last bit of air out of the atmosphere, but nature abhors a vacuum, and suddenly the chilled southwesterly wind arrived, initially as a whisper. Then it started to build.

For a few hours, it was benign enough, but just before midnight, the breeze began to whistle and shriek in the rigging, and all hands appeared on deck to tuck the mainsail's third reef to address the ever-

increasing loads on the mast and rigging. In the midst of the maneuver, with several of us on deck harnessed in and hanging on to the boom for dear life, David Thoreson came to a complete stop and grinned maniacally. "Welcome to the roaring forties," he quipped.

It was the beginning of a very, very long night.

The wind instruments aboard *Ocean Watch* provide wind strengths in true and apparent measurements—the former being the actual speed of the wind, and the latter its velocity when the boat's speed is factored in. But they also measure it according to the Beaufort Wind Force Scale, so named for Admiral Sir Francis Beaufort of the Royal Navy, who in 1805 devised a system to grade the wind's intensity on a scale of Force 1 to 12. Beaufort's scale, based mainly on visual sightings, was originally conceived to help frigate sailing masters determine how much canvas they could carry. As the breeze continued to strengthen, *Ocean Watch* sailed into a solid Force 8 gale (winds of 34 to 40 knots), flirting at times with Force 9 "strong gale" territory (41 to 47 knots, the top gust we registered).

According to the Beaufort Scale, here's what a Force 8 gale looks like: "Moderately high waves, longer (periods), edges of crests begin to break into spindrift. Well-marked streaks of foam." And Force 9: "High waves, dense streams of foam. Crests begin to topple, tumble, and roll over. Spray may affect visibility."

Luckily, it was dark out. Then, after a while, inevitably and sadly, it wasn't.

Daybreak was a double-edged sword. Yes, we'd made it through the night without breaking anything or anybody. But with dawn's early light, we could actually see what the heck was going on. In fact, the skies had cleared and were blue and sunny, putting everything into sharp focus.

Frankly, as far as we were concerned, Sir Beaufort's descriptions seemed understated. Winslow Homer could not have rendered a more dramatic seascape.

There was to all of this, in those brief philosophical moments that somehow come forth when frayed nerves are exposed to nature's raw power, a wild yet serene beauty to the scene: the wayward seas, the piercing illumination, the striking cerulean sky—this was what sailors call a fair-weather gale—and just for good measure, the unflappable albatrosses that had suddenly appeared out of nowhere. We understood that we'd weathered the worst of it.

As the day progressed, what was surprising about the overnight blow was its relatively gentle aftermath. When all the planets are in alignment, as we'd discovered during our summer above the Arctic Circle, voyaging in the high latitudes can be an almost addictive experience. We'd had a taste of what lured men like Roald Amundsen and others to the nether regions of the globe time and again.

And once the front had barreled out to sea, it was replaced by a massive high-pressure system easing off the coast of Patagonia, with gorgeous blue skies overhead and a pleasant northwesterly breeze filling in from astern. Conditions could not possibly have been sweeter. Furthermore, from the forecasts, it appeared the high had settled in for a while.

"Roaring forties?" Dave Logan wondered aloud at some point the next morning, just about the time his first cup of java kicked in. "This is more like the fantastic forties."

FOR THE BIRDS

While the weather was clear and the sailing fast, the temperatures began to plunge, and with each change of watch it seemed as if we were adding another layer of fleece or long underwear.

Just a few days earlier, we'd been bodysurfing off Mar del Plata in 68° F (28° C) waters that were fresh but not unpleasant. On January 8, the seawater temperature gauge registered 54° F (12° C). The trend was clear, as was the fact that we'd had our last swim for a while.

As the thermometer plunged, however, there was good news, too; the days became longer. The previous evening, twilight lingered until well past 10 PM; the waning moon rose two hours later; the morning sun arrived five hours after that. This time-elapsed celestial sequence made for a quick, merciful night, and the new day brought a steady progression of very welcome visitors.

For after a long, fallow spell with very few sightings of any sort, the wildlife had returned. We saw orcas and humpbacks, dolphins and basking sharks. But for the rest of the passage, day after day, hour after hour, what stopped us cold were the stately albatrosses, of which we spied several species, from mottled youths to confident adults. They seemed to be particularly enamored with the disturbed air off the leech of our mainsail, where they twirled and wheeled to our endless joy

Opposite page: A sea lion snoozes happily. *This page:* After bidding farewell to a sleepy friend in Punta del Este, the albatrosses and porpoises became frequent companions on our passage southward *(above and right)*. *Top:* Rookie offshore sailor Roxanne Nanninga described her experience as "à la carte sailing."

and amazement. But the ones that left the most indelible impressions were the grand, wandering albatrosses, their enormous 10-foot (3-m) wingspans practically locked in place, gliding and soaring between the wavelets with efficient, sparing effort, then jibing downwind on the thermals like a racing yacht angling toward the leeward mark.

As we dipped below 46° S, we enjoyed a peppy night of sailing, running wing-and-wing before breezes that hovered in the 20- to 25-knot range until the wee hours, when the steady northwesterly wind finally began to falter and veer to the west. We reset the sails accordingly and continued making good progress on a beam reach through much of the morning before the breeze quit altogether and we kicked the engine over.

A couple of uneventful days later, the new watch coming on deck at 6 AM was roused with an unusual order: "Bring your cameras."

Up forward, Captain Schrader was wedged into the bow pulpit, laughing out loud like a schoolkid on recess. Aft, our athletic photographer, Thoreson, was bouncing from beam to beam, light on his feet, working the angles like Muhammad Ali in his prime. Both were raising and lowering cameras: click, click, click.

That's because, quite literally, albatrosses surrounded them.

We'd been sailing in company with the riveting creatures for days, but usually in small groups and never more than a handful at a time. This was different. On a morning bathed in pristine light, there were

dozens and dozens of birds circling *Ocean Watch*. It was impossible to know which way to look. Lone gliders hovered inches atop the wavelets.

Small squadrons of five or six flyers tacked upwind in perfect alignment, in a formation as synchronized as anything the Blue Angels might do. Some were landing atop the ocean, an exercise not unlike sailing up to a mooring: point directly into the wind; luff the sails; stop forward motion; alight.

Perhaps not coincidentally, just five hours before on the morning of January 10, *Ocean Watch* slipped past the fiftieth parallel on the final approach to Stanley, the capital of the Falkland Islands. You could say those morning birds were a final gift, the icing on the cake. For

remarkably, with one relatively brief exception on that first agonizing night at sea, the dash through the roaring forties had in fact, contrary to expectations, been a glorious run blessed with a favorable breeze and the company of those albatrosses.

Contrary to old but conventional wisdom, it had been a lawful, orderly place. Yes, we had been slapped around harshly for those initial twenty-four hours, but in retrospect, it was a small price to pay for the fine trip that followed.

We exited the forties like gamblers leaving Vegas with pockets full of house money, and we didn't look behind us to see who or what might be giving chase. The Falklands were upon us.

Opposite page and top: In Mar del Plata, the mass of humanity packing the resort city's beaches left the skipper wondering if we were "loving our oceans to death." *Above:* Visiting scientists briefed us on the weather and currents we'd encounter en route to Cape Horn.

CHAPTER 10

FALKLAND ISLANDS INTERLUDE

A mong the many things for which the Falkland Islands are famous—the wildlife, the scenery, and unfortunately, the 1982 Argentine invasion that led to the Falklands War—is the changeable, confounding weather. We got a taste of it as we closed in on the remote archipelago in the exposed South Atlantic.

From 30 nautical miles out, under totally sunny skies, the islands ahead were covered in cumulus clouds. Moments later, we were doused by showers. They stopped, and the sun reappeared. Then it got cloudy again. Then rainy. Clear. Gray. Drizzly. When the skies finally parted for good and we could register our surroundings, the barren, brown, spooky landscape looked startlingly like the terrain above the Arctic Circle through the Northwest Passage.

Twenty-seven years earlier, on Mark Schrader's first solo circumnavigation aboard a Valiant 40 called *Resourceful*, he paid an unexpected call at Stanley with mechanical problems and had been treated royally by the engaging Falkland Islanders. He'd always wanted to return. As we neared Stanley, as usual when entering a new country, we raised the nation's courtesy flag, in this case Great Britain's Union Jack. "I want to make an impression coming in," said the skipper, as he hoisted it up the rigging.

On our final approach, with major ribbons of breeze honking down the outlying strait, Dave Logan steered *Ocean Watch* through the narrow cut into wide Stanley Harbor on East Falkland Island. We'd been granted permission to tie up at the docks of the Falkland Islands Company, but with an offshore breeze it would be a tricky landing. Luckily, at the last minute, out of nowhere appeared a helpful fellow in a red slicker. We heaved a line ashore, he got it around a bollard, and, thanks to his assistance, the docking maneuver went smoothly.

Our Good Samaritan was a company employee named Marcello, a fount of friendly information. When everyone had caught their breath, he looked at us sheepishly and said, "Only one thing. I just got a call from up the hill. That flag?" he said, pointing at the British ensign flapping in the breeze. "It's upside down."

We all gazed aloft, jaws slack. Who knew the Union Jack wasn't symmetrical? In any event, we Yankees had indeed made an indelible first impression, though not the one the skipper was hoping for.

And actually, we weren't an all-American crew. Argentine sailor Horacio Rosell had joined us in Mar del Plata to assist us with logistics on the next legs of the trip, where a Spanish-speaking crewman would prove to be invaluable. But given the history between the Brits and Argentines, we were anxious about how he'd be received. The customs agent who cleared us in quickly put everyone's mind at ease.

"Everyone is welcomed to the Falklands," he said. "Enjoy your stay." It set the tone for the entire visit.

Above: Those of us on board *Ocean Watch* found the king penguin colony at Volunteer Point enthralling. *Opposite page:* One of Falkland's 600,000 sheep cast a weary eye on the penguins' proceedings.

SURFING IN TUXEDOES

The original plan when we arrived in the Falklands was to spend a few days investigating some of the outer islands—there are more than two hundred in all, sprinkled between two main isles, East Falkland and West Falkland—but with gales raking the local waters for most of the week, it was prudent to remain dockside. Thankfully we did manage to take in some sights on East Falkland Island.

One morning, we piled into a 4x4 for the 7-mile (11-km) drive out to Gypsy Cove and Yorke Bay, the nearest places to downtown Stanley for scenic walks and wildlife sightings. Along the way, we saw a couple of shipwrecks, including the rusting hulk of the three-masted *Lady Elizabeth*, built of iron in the United Kingdom in 1879 and finished with duty in 1913 after clipping a shallow rock.

Once we'd hit the trail—and taken notice of the off-limits signs designating minefields that still haven't been cleared—we came upon the remnants of the gun station at Ordnance Point, one of fourteen manned defense sites during the war. In fact, evidence of the conflict over the sovereignty of the islands, which the Argentines still refer to as the Malvinas, was everywhere.

Gypsy Cove was a wild place, but it paled in comparison to our destination a day later, magnificent Volunteer Point, on the easternmost tip of the island. To get there, the skipper had lined up a pair of 4x4s. The long, mostly off-road drive out, across spongy, uneven tundra and muddy bogs, was a bone-jarring experience. But after a couple of long hours, we crested a small ridge, and the view ahead was no longer a wide plain of highly shaky terrain but a breathtaking expanse of sandy, white beach. With the wind blowing the tops off the endless sets of steep, greenish-blue rollers, it was obvious the pounding had been worth it.

On the drive out, we'd seen a goodly sample of the Falkland's 600,000 sheep, but we'd endured the ride to Volunteer Point to visit the largest king penguin colony in the islands. Other birds, including steamer ducks, thrushes, rock shags, skuas, and geese, and a couple of other penguin species also reside there: the Magellanic—known locally as jackasses—and the Gentoo.

There are more than a thousand breeding adult king penguins in the colony, and they raise more than five hundred chicks annually. Unlike the skittish Gentoo and jackass penguins, the kings weren't bothered by our presence. After an afternoon of wandering around with them, we all had our favorite stories. Logan spied a protective parent wallop a skua edging in on a chick. David Thoreson watched a trio try to negotiate the long step from a sand dune down to the beach, without luck, until one decided to take the leap and tumbled forward like a felled tree.

However, once in the surf, all signs of clumsiness disappeared. Entering the water, the jackass penguins almost burrowed into the first

Above: A rocky point marked the entrance to Stanley.
Opposite page: The three-masted *Lady Elizabeth* was one of countless shipwrecks we saw, and reminders of the Falklands War were everywhere. *Following pages:* The stirring sunset on our last night in the islands was a good omen.

PORT PLEASANT'S WAR MEMORIAL SHOCKED OUR ARGENTINE MATE, WHO QUESTIONED THE INVASION OF THE COUNTRY.

WARNING

ALTHOUGH THIS AREA IS BELIEVED TO BE CLEAR OF MINES, IT IS POSSIBLE THAT A MINE MAY BE WASHED ASHORE FROM A NEARBY MINEFIELD. PLEASE BE CAREFUL. DO NOT TOUCH ANY SUSPICIOUS OBJECT, BUT PLACE A MARKER NEARBY AND REPORT IT TO THE JSEODOC, STANLEY.

shallow waves, with fins in full flutter mode. Once clear of that initial break, they flashed underwater at incredible speed. Every once in a while, we'd see one leap and dive, doing its best imitation of a porpoise. But mostly they swam, fast and free, their sleek black bodies sliding below the surface like living torpedoes. My own lasting memory was of some penguins I saw in full bodysurfing mode, nestled in the curl. On the voyage around the Americas, we'd seen some amazing wildlife, but I'll never forget the sight of those penguins, those natural surfers, slashing through the waves.

PLEASANT OMENS

On January 18, after a weeklong stay in the fine and friendly town of Stanley, the crew of *Ocean Watch* sailed out of Stanley Harbor and set a course for the protected waters of Port Pleasant a few hours away. Once there, we dropped the anchor off a small inlet called Fitzroy Creek and launched the dinghy and kayaks to have a look at the deserted cluster of buildings known as Fitzroy Settlement. It was quiet and peaceful, which made a passage from Ewen Southby-Tailyour's excellent cruising

guidebook, *Falkland Island Shores*, all the more eerie.

"It was in Fitzroy Creek," noted Southby-Tailyour, "that the two Royal Fleet Auxiliary ships the *Sir Galahad* and the *Sir Tristam* were anchored on the morning of 8 June 1982 when they were hit by Argentinian aircraft, with the worst single casualty list of the whole campaign. The ships were anchored west of Pleasant Island and due south of the settlement."

So was *Ocean Watch*. We'd seen what appeared to be a small graveyard and the unmistakable war memorial upon arriving in the bay. Like the ruins of the fortress we'd toured in the Aleutian Islands, it gave us pause. Our Argentine mate, Horacio Rosell, was particularly moved.

"What were we thinking?" he said.

However, as evening drew near, the sun truly broke for the first time since we'd arrived in the Falklands, and we were stunned by perhaps the best sunset of the voyage thus far. It seemed like a good omen. So, too, did the school of Peale's dolphins that accompanied us as we got under way the next morning. It was getting to be high summer in the high southern seas. That meant it was high time to set sail for Cape Horn.

LESSONS LEARNED ALONG THE WAY

The Around the Americas expedition was conceived as a voyage of discovery, and from the Northwest Passage to the tip of South America, the crew continuously learned new lessons about the environment, ocean conservation, oceanography, and other scientific disciplines. But a big part of the mission—in lectures, presentations, boat tours, and school visits—was to pass on what we'd discovered to students, sailors, scientists, and the scores of everyday folks we met along the way. Almost always, the most instructional encounters were the unexpected ones.

1) On Cooper Island in the Northwest Passage, ornithologist George Divoky described the changes he'd witnessed firsthand—to the ice, the climate, and the wildlife—during his ongoing studies of the black guillemots. 2) In the thriving scientific community of Barrow, Alaska, we hiked into the tundra to learn more about the ever-changing permafrost.

3) Oceanographer Michael Reynolds was an invaluable member of the crew, interpreting and explaining the natural world around us on a regular basis. 4) During our visit to Miami's Rosenstiel School of Marine and Atmospheric Science, we had a firsthand lesson on the dynamics of Biscayne Bay aboard the 96-foot (29-m) research vessel *F. G. Walton Smith.*

Power of One

5) Along with a curious youngster, we learned a few facts about sea turtles at the Hollings Marine Laboratory in Charleston, South Carolina. 6–7) Whether the crew was studying cloud formations or searching for sea life, *Ocean Watch* was an ideal platform for observation and reflection. 8) In New York City, we were able to share our knowledge of local waters with inner-city kids through the Power of One program.

9) Poring over ice charts in the Northwest Passage and learning to address and understand the dynamic sea ice both contributed to our ongoing education. 10) We assisted ice scientists in their studies by retrieving a previously deployed drift buoy that had beached itself on a remote Arctic barrier island. 11) Diving in the Spanish Virgin Islands, we investigated changes in the Caribbean Sea.

Picturing the Journey
CHAMPAGNE SAILING

After undergoing a complete pre-voyage refit in Seattle, the 64-foot (20-m) steel cutter _Ocean Watch_ proved to be the ideal vessel for long-range sailing from the high latitudes to the tropics and everywhere in between. Some of the best sailing of the entire circumnavigation came on the 600-nautical-mile run through the roaring forties.

In light to moderate winds, _Ocean Watch_ flew her working sails: full main, genoa, and staysail _(above left)_. Running before the wind, the crew would pole out the headsail to set the sails "wing and wing" _(top)_. Once the breeze began to howl, it was time to take a reef in the mainsail _(above)_. When conditions were ideal, _Ocean Watch_ reeled off the miles under the big asymmetrical spinnaker _(right)_.

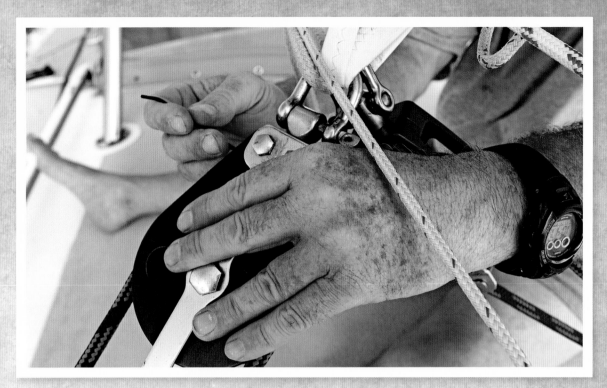

The crew employed some creative rope work to harness the power of the big asymmetric spinnaker (*opposite*). Oversized blocks and tackle were utilized to control the impressive loads on the sails and rigging (*top left*). When the wind truly howled, *Ocean Watch* sailed under a deeply reefed mainsail (*top right*). In lighter conditions, with the spinnaker full and drawing, the miles flew by (*above*).

PART 3

CAPE HORN
TO STARBOARD

CHAPTER 11
RACING THE WILLIWAWS

For many reasons, the waters in the high latitudes of South America have earned their reputation as a harsh, unforgiving cruising ground. These include the wicked currents and tides, the ferocious weather, the limited opportunities to seek and find shelter particularly in deteriorating conditions, and, finally, the amplification of the breeze off the tall Andes mountains.

These "amplified breezes," also known as williwaws, are powerful gusts of wind that rocket down the face of the steep peaks lining the coast, channels, and canals of South America beyond the fiftieth parallel. We did not doubt that *Ocean Watch* would be tested by the williwaws at some point.

We set forth from the Falkland Islands, bound for the famed Patagonian waters of the Beagle Channel and the Chilean naval town of Puerto Williams, nestled along its shores, that would serve as our staging area for Cape Horn. Before long, it became apparent that our first bout with the local williwaws might come sooner rather than later. Once under way, we had 360 nautical miles of open Atlantic Ocean to cross before we'd reach the relatively enclosed and protected anchorages of Beagle Channel. As we set a course eastward, however, we began tracking a strong gale swooping in from the west.

All signs pointed to the likelihood that the storm and *Ocean Watch* would converge in roughly two days right at the mouth of the channel. If we managed to beat the blow there, we could be safely anchored before the worst of it. If not, we'd be vulnerable to another pasting. Simply put, we'd be racing the williwaws.

At this point, two significant obstacles stood between *Ocean Watch* and the goal of a safe harbor. The first, due east of the peninsula known as Tierra del Fuego near the southern terminus of South America, was a craggy, current-swept isle known in local parlance as Isla de los Estados. To gringos like us, it was Staten Island. But by far the more ominous gateway was the narrow, 16-nautical-mile body of water separating the island and the continent—a messy, roiling cauldron of southerly current that can funnel through the passage at anywhere from 4 to 8 knots—called the Strait of Le Maire.

STATEN ISLAND FERRY

In their comprehensive cruising tome, *Patagonia and Tierra del Fuego Nautical Guide*, Italian sailors and authors Mariolina Rolfo and Giorgio Ardrizzi comment on the Strait of Le Maire and surrounding waters, saying: "Even in good weather, one is never sure to pass unmolested."

Above and opposite page: The craggy peaks and rocky outcroppings at remote Staten Island looked like something from another planet and signaled our impending date with the notorious Strait of Le Maire.

Obviously, in dicey conditions—say, when the southerly current slams into strong northerly winds, creating what the writers describe as "10-meter [33-foot] tidal overfalls and vicious standing waves"—the odds on molestation increase exponentially.

Suddenly, we realized, the williwaws might be the least of our problems. But before we'd tackle the strait, our big steel ferry—*Ocean Watch*—needed to negotiate the dangerous shores of Staten Island.

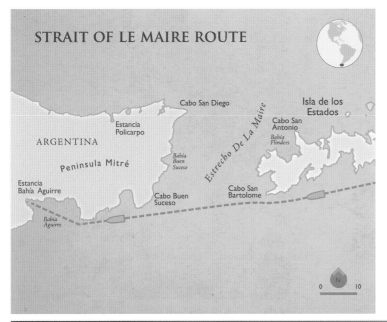

Just more than twenty-four hours after leaving the Falkland Islands, sailing fast and well, *Ocean Watch* was positioned roughly 90 nautical miles east of Staten Island, right in the heart of the furious fifties. The previous night, as the breeze kicked up over 30 knots, it appeared the place would live up to its reputation.

Luckily for us, however, the truly snotty winds and bouncy attendant seaway were mercifully brief, and soon gave way to a starry night and winds in the 20-knot range. "The fitful fifties," said Logan. Soon after daybreak, the sun appeared; a school of southern right whales rolled by; the wind swung just north of west; and it appeared we were negotiating the friendly fifties.

But the only true constant in the deep Southern Ocean is change, and we knew it was coming, just not exactly what it would be. The race to the Beagle Channel was well and truly on.

Isla de los Estados, or Staten Island, was given its name in 1615 by the Dutch merchant mariner Willem Schouten, master of a ship called *Eendracht*, who called the isle and the surrounding territory Her Staten Land (the Land of Their Lords) after his sovereign patrons and benefactors. Likewise, the Strait of Le Maire was named for another expedition backer, ship owner Isaac Le Maire.

More notably, Schouten will also go down in history as the man who named Cape Horn: the *Hoorn* was one of the ships in his armada and was also the name of the Dutch town from which he'd departed some eight months previous.

Above: Midway across the Strait of Le Maire, the trip became even more exciting when *Ocean Watch* rendezvoused with an anticipated front. *Opposite page, clockwise from top left:* Once into Bahía Aguirre, the weather cleared and we enjoyed a quiet night in the enclosed cove after witnessing a rainbow.

At 3 in the morning on January 20, the first purplish hint of dawn was visible to the southeast, and the looming presence of Her Staten Land was cloaked in shadowy mist to the northwest, with *Ocean Watch* sandwiched in between. Skipper Schrader and first mate Logan had logged long stretches at the navigation station formulating a strategy. The best places to seek shelter on Staten Island in a northerly gale, surprisingly, are along the deeply indented northern shore—if you get there before the weather socks in. But a northern approach could mean slipping into the Strait of Le Maire afterward, in a dreaded wind-against-tide scenario. A southern end run around Staten, in the island's lee, was deemed the sounder tactic.

We'd made decent time from the Falkland Islands to Staten's eastern flank, but that was about to end. By 4:30 AM, we were pounding dead upwind in a 30-knot westerly, bucking a foul current that would soon rise to more than 2.5 knots, and making just over 3 knots.

It was the beginning of yet another very long day. On the bright side, our slow pace in the emerging morning light gave us a good, close look at the 40-mile-long (65-km-long) island.

"Craggy," said Logan. I was thinking "saw-toothed." Either way, compared with the flat Falklands, we were now in the Himalayas. Sunrise was spectacular. The reflected light on the jagged mountains cast a rosy hue across the summits, some of which were flecked with patches of snow.

By 9 AM, the wind died altogether. But the afternoon forecast remained worrisome: "Gale warning with dangerous seas. Small-craft advisory. Use extreme caution. Moderate short-period wind waves. Winds: NNW 27 to 36 knots. Seas: NNW 6 feet @ 5 seconds." In the still conditions, Staten was an arresting visage; birds were everywhere, including a variety of tiny penguins we hadn't seen before, bobbing in and out of the water. The sky to the west, however, began to look bleak, and the barometer was in free fall. But we could see the end of west Staten Island—it looked like a mini Cape Horn—and a gray promontory farther beyond. South America.

A little after 11 AM, out from the island's lee, we unrolled the jib and stuck our toe into the Strait of Le Maire. The wind was building but from a good direction, to the north of west.

About a third of the way across the strait, the breeze rose into the mid-20-knot range, and we careened along at a somewhat frantic 10 knots, so we rolled up the genoa in a cold rain and replaced it with the staysail. We were, as we'd say on good sailing days, hauling the mail. For most of the trip across the strait, a big cell of precipitation hovered right over us. Then, with the entrance to the channel in sight, it burst open.

Down went the staysail; in went the third reef in the main. On deck, the breeze had risen into the mid-30-knot range; the air was cold and wet. We'd just sailed south of 55° S. Major gusts of wind ramping down the steep mountain faces were coursing down the channel just as we tucked out of the Strait of Le Maire and into the shadow of the peninsula. The williwaws had won.

The last hour, naturally, was the wildest. A Force 9 gale pummeling down the channel blew the tops of waves sideways in gusts to 50 knots. We yanked down the mainsail and made for a deep cove called Bahía Aguirre.

At the end of the day, the sun finally broke through the clouds, revealing a vast, intriguing landscape of hills and *estancias*, or farming

Opposite page: The rusting hulk of the *Micalvi*, once a Chilean naval vessel, was a well-known watering hole. *This page:* The *Ocean Watch* crew was invited into a "secret" society known as the Brotherhood of the Coast *(top)*, and the skipper was honored with a special chapeau *(middle)*. From Puerto Williams, another yacht set out for Cape Horn *(above)*.

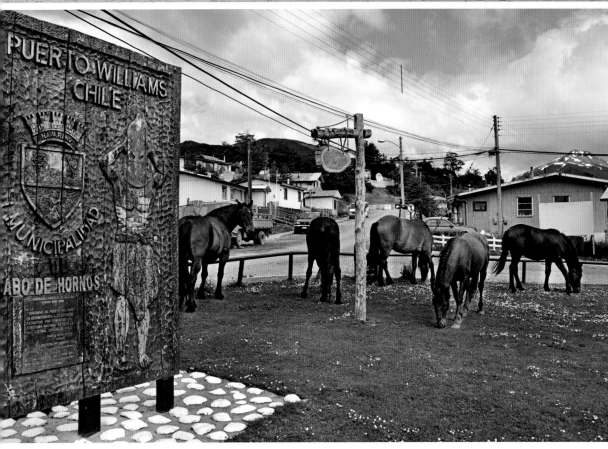

Above: Puerto Williams is characterized by horses roaming around town.
Top and right: This navy town nestles against a dramatic backdrop.

estates. As we motored into the bay, the front rolled out to sea and a vivid rainbow emerged. The ensuing sunset was accompanied by a series of astounding cloud formations that we found to be as changeable and hypnotizing as the northern lights.

FOLLOWING THE *BEAGLE*

The Beagle Channel—a winding, snake-like, 150-nautical-mile waterway that links the Atlantic Ocean, to the east, with the Pacific Ocean, to the west—was named after the HMS *Beagle* during its first hydrographic survey of the coasts and islands of Patagonia and Tierra del Fuego between the years of 1826 and 1830.

It was the *Beagle's* second voyage, however, that etched its name into the annals of history, science, and exploration. For it was on this return journey that Captain Robert FitzRoy employed the services of an amateur naturalist named Charles Darwin as a gentleman's companion, and to help with documenting the geography and natural history of the areas the crew visited.

Darwin turned out to have a meticulous eye. His careful observations of the natural world around him brought him some note back home, and became the foundation of his considered thoughts on natural selection and the theory of evolution.

On January 29, 1833, Darwin himself sailed into the Beagle Channel for the very first time and in his own brand of shorthand jotted this in his field notebook: "Many glaciers beryl blue most beautiful contrasted with snow."

On January 21, some 177 years later, *Ocean Watch* followed Darwin into the Beagle for the first time on the journey Around the Americas. If Darwin were with us, this is what he might've penned: "Snow-capped mountains, birds a-flutter, as lovely a day as you'll see."

Very early that morning, *Ocean Watch* was under way for the 60-nautical-mile trip to Puerto Williams. The visual treats continued all day, starting with the leaping dolphins that followed us out of the bay, moving on to the blazing sunrise, and continuing with the flock of cormorants that signaled our precise entrance to the channel a few miles down the track—all punctuated by the snowy mountaintops and stark, unforgiving terrain as we slid down the channel's well-defined corridor en route to Puerto Williams.

As the afternoon progressed, a solid westerly breeze filled in. But it faltered in the final miles, and when we sailed into Puerto Williams and took a mooring near the famous bar on the shipwrecked Chilean naval vessel, the *Micalvi*, the waters were still and reflective.

Next stop? Cape Horn.

Above: In the long, luminescent twilight, the crew of *Ocean Watch* knew that they had reached distant Patagonia.

CHAPTER 12

ISLA HORNOS

It is a place of maritime myth and lore, celebrated in tales, verse, and song. As South America's southernmost bit of land, the one and only Cape Horn is a speck on the chart of the vast Southern Ocean at 55°58'47" S by 67°16'18" W. Situated on a hardscrabble slab of rock called Isla Hornos, in the Hermite Islands group, Cape Horn forms the tip of this isolated island at the southern terminus of the fabled Tierra del Fuego archipelago.

Cape Horn has been called the Mount Everest of offshore sailing, and the list of voyagers who've sailed long and hard to gaze upon it is storied and select: Sir Francis Drake, Vito Dumas, Bernard Moitessier, Sir Francis Chichester, Robin Knox-Johnston, and, yes, Mark Schrader, among others. On January 22, 2010, *Ocean Watch* set sail for it.

Just one day after arriving in Puerto Williams, Chile, following a robust passage from the Falkland Islands, the 64-foot (20-m) cutter set forth on the single-most significant leg of the entire expedition around the Americas—namely, the rounding of Cape Horn. The crew had arrived with plans to wait as long as necessary for an ideal weather window, but as it turned out, it was a brief pause. David Thoreson, who was our onboard meteorologist in addition to photographer and watch captain, had been tracking the weather for more than a week. He wrote in the immediate hours after clearing Chilean customs:

As Ocean Watch arrived in Puerto Williams, there appeared to be two small weather windows existing to head south to Cape Horn in northwesterly gales. This has been apparent now for the last few days, but the problem then becomes, "What next?"

This question develops because of the tremendous west to east directional airflow, and this week is no exception with gales forecasted for four of the next six days.

Using the gale from the west-northwest to leave Puerto Williams and head south to an anchorage close to the Horn positions us close enough to then take advantage of a directional change or decrease in pressure.

Tomorrow afternoon (January 23) brings a forecasted wind of WNW 10 to 15 knots on both the east and west sides of the Horn. This is the weather window to take our shot before the south and westerly gales kick right back in overnight.

In other words, the window was open, and the long-term forecast suggested that once it closed—when the parade of westerly gales that were also prominently featured on the weather maps began marching through—it might be weeks before we'd enjoy such a favorable meteorological picture.

Above: Buffeted by high winds on the way to Cape Horn, the crew was rewarded by a rare easterly breeze—and set their spinnaker *(opposite page)*—while rounding the famous landmark, shrouded in mist.

Of course, as we set sail from Puerto Williams, we had no clue that much of the short-term forecast was pure fiction.

CHASING HISTORY

The first European sailors to lay eyes on the Horn may well have been Sir Francis Drake and his crew. In the fall of 1578, Drake sailed through the Strait of Magellan and into the Pacific Ocean. Before he got very far, a vicious northerly filled in, and Drake was blown southward, toward Antarctica. South of Tierra del Fuego, he realized that the archipelago was not another continent, as believed at the time, but instead was a group of islands—including Isla Hornos—that bordered an open sea. That expanse of water between the Horn and Antarctica is today known as Drake Passage, an enduring epitaph for his troubles.

It was almost forty years later, in January 1616, that the Dutch merchant mariner Willem Schouten set out for the South Atlantic in search of a new route to the Far East. Schouten commanded two ships, the *Eendracht* and the *Hoorn*, the latter of which was shipwrecked en route. *Eendracht* carried forth by herself, and in late January, almost 394 years to the day before *Ocean Watch*'s Horn attempt, Schouten found what he'd been looking for. This excerpt from the ship's log tells the story:

In the evening 25 January 1616 the winde was South West, and that night wee went South with great waves or billowes out of the southwest, and very blew water, whereby wee judged, and held for certaine that . . . it was the great South Sea, whereat we

were exceeding glad to thinke that wee had discovered a way, which until that time, was unknowne to men, as afterward wee found it to be true.

On 29 January 1616 we saw land againe lying northwest and north northwest from us, which was the land that lay South from the straights of Magellan which reacheth Southward, all high hillie lande covered over with snow, ending with a sharpe point which wee called Kaap Hoorn [Cape Horn] . . .

Especially through the Great Age of Sail from the 1700s to the early 1900s, Cape Horn was a significant waypoint on the well-traveled clipper routes for the grand square rigs that carried much of the world's trade. The hard men who drove those ships were called Cape Horners, and for them swimming was not considered a useful skill. The idea was that if they went overboard in those godforsaken seas, it was thought better to get it over with quickly.

The first yachtsman to sail these waters was the crusty American solo sailor Joshua Slocum. Slocum was the first man to sail around the world alone, and he visited Tierra del Fuego—where he famously scattered carpet tacks across his deck to dissuade the natives from boarding—in 1895. But it's unclear whether he actually rounded Cape Horn.

There is no doubt, however, about Conor O'Brien, who successfully negotiated Cape Horn aboard his 42-foot (13-m) *Saoirse* in the early 1920s. The great Argentine navigator Vito Dumas was the first man to sail around the world alone via the Horn, in 1942. The

Above and above center: On the way south, a shipwreck reminded us of the need to be careful, while the sea life and their endless surprises reminded us of what an intriguing journey we were on.

renowned English aviator and navigator Francis Chichester earned a knighthood in 1966 for circling the globe solo, past Cape Horn, with a single layover in Australia. And another British legend, Robin Knox-Johnston, was the first to accomplish the feat without stopping when he won the Golden Globe Race in the late 1960s.

No one ever did a better job of romanticizing the place than the Frenchman Bernard Moitessier, who rounded the cape twice and wrote a pair of books about the experience that inspired generations of young French adventurers. Ever since, French sailors have dominated marathon single-handed races and crewed round-the-world records around Cape Horn. In fact, our own Mark Schrader was the first American to circle the planet alone via the five great southern capes—including the Horn—in 1982.

This time, Schrader had plenty of company: a crew of eight, our biggest since leaving Seattle. Along with the core crew of four, the team included our translator, Horacio Rosell; Sailors for the Sea founder David Rockefeller Jr. and cofounder and board member David Treadway, both of whom came aboard in Puerto Williams; and accomplished long-distance sailor and another Sailors for the Sea board member, Ned Cabot, who'd joined the boat in the Falkland Islands.

In the Chilean channels, the Chilean Armada, as the country's navy is called, closely monitors the movements of all vessels, insisting upon regular position updates via VHF radio on a twice-daily basis.

AS WE SET SAIL FROM PUERTO WILLIAMS, WE HAD NO CLUE THAT THE SHORT-TERM FORECAST WAS PURE FICTION.

Top: (From left): David Rockefeller, Mark Schrader, David Treadway, and Ned Cabot were key members of the Cape Horn team. *Above:* During a break in the action, Cabot tended to a shore-side blaze. *Following pages:* As we closed in on the Horn, conditions deteriorated.

Rosell handled all our communications flawlessly. We were also lucky to receive the valuable advice of Rockefeller's friend and seasoned Chilean sailing expert, Augustine "Doonie" Edwards—who happened to be in the midst of his own Cape Horn expedition aboard his 80-foot (24-m) ketch, *Gloriana*.

RISING WINDS

After clearing customs and formally registering our intentions with the Chilean Armada, the plan was to sail roughly 90 nautical miles south of Puerto Williams to Isla Herschel, a small island just north of Isla Hornos. On the northwest flank of Herschel, off an enclosed body of water called Bahía Arquistade, was a protected anchorage called Caleta Martial that looked like a good place to regroup.

A fine breeze was pumping down the narrow Beagle Channel, the boundaries of which are lined by a string of rolling, snow-capped mountains. Rockefeller remarked that the channel and the peaks reminded him of Juneau, Alaska, and I realized he was right. It was windy, perhaps 25 knots, but out of the right direction, funneling over *Ocean Watch*'s transom, and it was about to get breezier.

Isla Navarino is the major island in this section of the archipelago, and before long *Ocean Watch* slid inside Isla Picton and through a pair of passes, Paso Picton and Paso Goree. By now, the breeze was pumping into the mid-30s, with gusts to 40 knots. Sailing under staysail alone, *Ocean Watch* was making good progress, but soon even the tiny headsail was too much, and the skipper called for a change down to the storm staysail. Dolphins frolicked in the bow wave, albatrosses spun and twirled, and groups of Magellanic penguins popped up alongside to pay their respects.

It was about to get windier still.

Out from the lee of Navarino and into the expansive bay called Bahía Nassau, the breeze really started to whistle, locked into the high 30s with gusts well above 40 knots. *Ocean Watch* plowed through wave after wave, and gray water continuously swept her decks. But she'd already proven to us on countless occasions that she reveled in such conditions, and every time she was drenched in a torrent of ocean, she just shook herself off and kept right on going.

It was wet and raw, but appropriate, too. Sailing to Cape Horn wasn't supposed to be easy. And then it got more difficult. As one small, self-contained weather cell after another raked the seas—and, of course,

Ocean Watch—the Hermite Islands appeared suddenly out of the mist. Forceful puffs of wind screamed down the inclines of the jagged isles—hello again, williwaws—whipping the water into a marbled, streaky tempest, and sometimes even spinning up small, isolated funnels of mini-waterspouts.

Between breaks in the squalls, low rainbows cascaded along the horizon, disappearing when the rain resumed. It was gusting into the 50s, perhaps even the 60s, and was certainly the most wind we'd seen in more than 18,000 nautical miles of sailing. Even the tiny storm staysail overpowered the boat. We scrambled forward to douse it as solid sheets of water cascaded over the foredeck.

Only later did we learn that while we were wrestling to tame the staysail, which flailed and flapped like something untamed and alive, the lighthouse keeper at Cape Horn recorded a gust of 105 knots. In the moment, however, it was information best unknown.

Then, finally, we slipped into Bahía Arquistade, and there just ahead was *Gloriana*, riding on two anchors, still and steady. Logan skillfully nestled *Ocean Watch* alongside an empty navy mooring nearby so we could run a pair of thick lines through the pad eye. Suddenly the commotion was over, at least for the moment; we'd found shelter from the storm. And Cape Horn was less than 10 nautical miles south.

In writer Dallas Murphy's book, *Rounding the Horn*, he captured something of the sense of what we collectively felt:

> All mariners since Magellan have recognized that when their bows crossed the Fortieth Parallel, they were entering an ocean entirely different from all the rest. Everything was exaggerated, accelerated in the "Roaring Forties" and the "Screaming Fifties." Big wind came on harder, faster, than on any other oceans . . .
>
> Even the look of the Southern Ocean was different from the rest: gray, grim, death colors. But there were also those explosions of light when for a time, the low murk parted and shafts of splendid brightness shone on the white crests like a hint of hope, and sometimes multiple rainbows arced across the horizon, intersecting.
>
> The fatigue, pain, and danger were all magnified, but so, too, was the magnificence of this ocean and its wildness . . .

Once again, it was a long evening, as the wind continued to howl with gusts into the 50s. At one stage, after midnight, one of our mooring lines parted, and it took the better part of two hours to sort out the mess and secure *Ocean Watch* once more. The next morning wasn't much better, but with a tight schedule to adhere to, at midday, with the breeze having settled into the mid-30-knot range, our Chilean friends on *Gloriana* hauled their anchors and made for the Horn.

However, with a more favorable forecast for the following day, January 24—easterly winds shifting southwest at 10 to 20 knots—we decided to wait another day for even better conditions. Late that afternoon, we left Isla Herschel and motored a few miles to an anchorage off Isla Wollaston, which looked from the charts as if it would provide better protection. Our updated plan—always subject to change, but in keeping with the itinerary we'd presented to the Chilean Armada—was to rise very early on January 24, round Cape Horn, and continue straight back to Puerto Williams.

CABO DE HORNOS

According to the *Pilot Charts*, the month-by-month statistical analysis of winds and weather for all of the world's oceans, the odds on seeing an easterly breeze in January off the tip of South America were exceedingly long. For weeks, we'd been obsessing over forecasts for this region, and it wasn't until the day before that it had come up in even the briefest of mentions. But none of us were buying it. So we were still wondering what lay ahead when we raised our own anchor and set out from Wollaston at the stroke of 5 AM on January 24.

For the record, from Wollaston we made our way into Bahía Scourfield; through the Canal Bravo bisecting Isla Wollaston and Isla Freycinet; into Bahía Arquistade east of Isla Herschel; and finally through one last, narrow pass called Paso al Mar del Sur, just to the west of Isla Deceit. And then, there were no more islands. Except one: Isla Hornos.

Cape Horn.

As with the Northwest Passage ice, at the Horn, nature—not your desires—dictates your movements. But from the first stages of planning the Around the Americas voyage, the skipper had hoped to tackle Cape Horn from east to west: Thematically, it played in harmony with the overall, clockwise circuit of the continents. Plus, he'd never done it before.

Successfully negotiating the Horn is never a given, and we all would've been very satisfied if the weather gods had served up nothing but heavy westerly winds and we'd tackled it from west to east. But as we closed in on Isla Hornos, we realized that the most recent forecast was correct, and waiting an extra day had paid off. We had our easterly.

It was dank, gray, and chilly, and the top end of the island—the famous edifice of the Horn—was shrouded in a foreboding cloak of cloud, fog, and mist. In other words, it was perfect.

"Well," said Thoreson, "it looks like a Cape Horn day."

Did it ever.

We sailed around the back side of Isla Hornos under triple-reefed main and staysail, the boat balanced and fast. When Schrader mentioned that we should get the spinnaker ready, Logan and I exchanged "he's got to be kidding" looks. But the moment passed.

Suddenly we were around the bend; we could see the lighthouse and the big monument on the high hill; holy smokes, there was Cabo de Hornos.

Cape Horn.

It's hard to describe the sensation of actually gazing at the Horn from seaward, from the deck of a small boat. We'd all seen the photos, of course, and several of us had been there before, but nothing short of staring at the bloody thing does it justice.

As a sailor, you instinctively realize you're slipping through waters both hallowed and lethal. You turn your head one way and see the iconic headland; turn it the other and see nothing but endless ocean. It's been said that Cape Horn looks like the end of the Earth, and you think, well, that's kind of trite. But, in fact, it really did look like the absolute, final, nonnegotiable end of the Earth.

Albatrosses by the dozen soared overhead. We cracked a couple of beers, poured a tot in the sea in homage to King Neptune, and then splashed another on the deck of *Ocean Watch*, the stout and sturdy vessel that had watched over us so carefully and for so long.

Rockefeller disappeared below and reemerged in shorts and a sport shirt. We all blinked and laughed. His fellow mates from Sailors for the

During the Great Age of Sail from the 1700s to the early 1900s, many a ship came to grief off Cape Horn *(opposite page, bottom)*, but some of the crew from this dismasted square-rigger took to a lifeboat and survived. In heavy weather, decks awash in boarding seas were a common occurrence *(above)*.

Sea, Treadway and Cabot, each took turns steering the boat. It's not every day you sail around Cape Horn.

We each, silently and to each other, in turns, invoked the names of family, friends, and fellow sailors whom we'd call or email later on, and more important, of those who'd journeyed to the great beyond, who would've been just as amazed by what we were witnessing, by what was transpiring, as we were.

It was the sort of place for that. We counted our blessings and hugged our "brothers": none of us would've made it to this wild spot that so few are privileged to see without one another.

"I always thought of this as just a rock. I had no great desire to get here," said Logan. "But I have to say, this is something."

It sure was. In a moment of inspiration, Logan went below and switched on the water maker, without letting it fully flush out beforehand. "It'll be a little briny," he said. "We'll all have a little Cape Horn water coursing through our veins."

With the following 15- to 20-knot southeasterly still holding, the skipper proved he wasn't kidding about the spinnaker. Once everything was rigged, he gave the nod and *Ocean Watch*'s big kite was hoisted and sheeted home. The numbers were all in sync: it was precisely 8 AM, right at 56° S, marking 18,300 nautical miles sailed since leaving Seattle.

Once the huge sail was full and drawing, *Ocean Watch*—and for that matter, all of us—were truly in our element. Grabbing cameras, we tried to capture the image of South America on the sail against the actual tip of South America right there before us.

All too soon, a squall appeared on the horizon, and we doused the spinnaker quickly, laughing and grinning at the outlandishness of the whole thing, like teenagers out past curfew. Surely we'd gotten away with something—and what a souvenir.

Of all the sailors on all the boats who have ever rounded the legendary southern waypoint of Cape Horn, few if any had ever done so from east to west while flying a billowing white spinnaker emblazoned with a glorious blue representation of the continents of North and South America. And even more significant, without doubt, none had ever done so, in either direction, just mere months after successfully negotiating the Northwest Passage.

Above: The "back side" of Isla Hornos was daunting and remote.
Opposite page: (top) Heading south into dangerous, rocky waters, the skipper found a moment for contemplation on the bow *(center)*.

On top of everything else, once we were truly south of Cape Horn—having already sailed to the westernmost, northernmost, and easternmost points of our circumnavigation of the Americas—we were now at the southernmost extent of our journey. In honor of the moment, Schrader went below and, as he had at each previous milestone, tossed a beautiful glass float—crafted by the renowned artist Dale Chihuly, who'd supported the expedition from its inception—into the ocean. It was one last tribute to the sea.

Five months earlier, high above the Arctic Circle, we'd turned into Navy Board Inlet at the northern reaches of Baffin Island and headed south. Ever since, the compass needle had pointed in a southerly direction, down the Labrador Sea, along the eastern seaboard, across the equator, past the endless coastline of Brazil and the rest of South America: south, south, south, south, south.

Now, as Chihuly's float bobbed astern, and with Cape Horn receding in our wake, Logan swung the wheel to starboard, and the compass spun in obedient assent.

We were headed north.

CHAPTER 13
IN PATAGONIA

When Skipper Mark Schrader envisioned the Around the Americas expedition, the original plan after rounding Cape Horn was to forge on "outside" the canals and waterways of Patagonia. *Ocean Watch* would then travel the open Pacific Ocean to the Chilean city of Puerto Montt, nearly 1,000 nautical miles to the north. But given that a series of powerful gales were screaming in from the west, rendering the entire route up the coast a dangerous lee shore, discretion overruled valor. We altered course for the inside option via the Beagle Channel, the Strait of Magellan, and a vast network of interconnected gulfs, canals, and waterways.

It proved to be a fortuitous, instructive choice. Had we chosen the offshore passage, we would've missed countless scenes of beauty, as well as the chance to see firsthand the threats and challenges to the waters, wildlife, and people of Southern Chile, Tierra del Fuego, and Patagonia.

But first, we returned to Puerto Williams for a brief layover to catch our breath after the exhilarating but strenuous rounding of Cape Horn. There, a surprise waited for us.

It's perhaps fitting that the first people to inhabit the region were the nomadic "canoe Indians" known as the Yaghans, who arrived in Patagonia some six thousand years ago. Sadly, the last of the resilient Yaghan descendents disappeared only recently, but anyone who ventures far in small boats can relate to their spirit and connection to the sea.

Today, the local channel pilots, fishermen, and other seamen who live by and work on the ocean can understand that affinity and are also vitally connected to the water. In fact, a wide-ranging group of such like-minded souls exists in South America, and they call themselves the Brotherhood of the Coast.

Apparently, in Uruguay, a member of the Brotherhood had found our voyage compelling. Back in Puerto Williams, our trusty Argentine crewman Horacio Rosell informed us that the local chapter of the Brotherhood would be picking us up that evening and taking us to an undisclosed location, the purposes of which remained unclear.

Arriving at a house on the outskirts of town, we felt like figures out of a mob movie, about to become "made men." Inside the house, a group of bandana-clad men wielding machetes awaited our arrival. No, we weren't joining the mafia, but we were indeed about to be inducted into a secret, closed society.

It was a night of speeches, songs, and camaraderie. When we were finally dropped back at *Ocean Watch* late that evening, we, too, wore pirate bandanas, except for the skipper, whose peaked hat looked like something out of the movie *Master and Commander*.

We'd had more than a few evenings to remember in our journey, at sea and ashore, but none of us will ever forget the night when we were accepted into the Brotherhood.

Once in the Beagle Channel (*above*), the Darwin Cordillera, a range of nearly 8,000-foot (2,438-m) mountains, provided jaw-dropping scenery (*opposite page*).

OF THE FORTY-
EIGHT GLACIERS
IN THE SOUTHERN
PATAGONIAN ICE
FIELDS, ALL BUT
TWO ARE RAPIDLY
SHRINKING.

INTO ANOTHER WORLD

After a day of hunkering down in port while winds of 30 to 40 knots swept Patagonia, on January 27 we set out into the Beagle Channel. It was worth the short wait.

We were under way at 5 AM, the breeze having exhausted itself. Our first impression of the Beagle was that we'd wandered into the Alps, if the Alps were bisected by a 150-nautical-mile channel of water that ran from deep, roiled blue to milky, glacial green.

Heading west from Puerto Williams, the first major feature was the Argentine city of Ushuaia, population sixty thousand, that sprawled along the shoreline as a long, wide shelf of civilization. It would be the last we'd see in a while. Geographically, the westward channel winds past a narrow waterway called the Canal Murray and the Peninsula Dumas, to port, before coming to a bold headland on the eastern flank of Isla Gordon called, appropriately enough, Punta Divide. To the north the Beagle is known as the Brazo Noroeste ("Northwest Arm"); to the south it is the Brazo Sudoeste ("Southwest Arm").

Ocean Watch went north, into another world.

The primary feature of the Northwest Arm of the Beagle is the Darwin Cordillera, a jaw-dropping range of nearly 8,000-foot (2,438-m) mountains bordered by *ventisqueros*, or glaciers, such as the Italia, Espana, and (most famous of all) Romanche. They came forth relentlessly: blue, angular, and unforgettable.

Thoreson, who'd traversed these waters in the 1990s, noticed a downside to the view: The alpine glaciers in the Chilean and Argentine

Opposite page, bottom: As in the Arctic, the ice in Southern Patagonia is changing. *Opposite page, top:* Perhaps the most famous of all the Chilean glaciers is the one called Romanche. ***This page, above:*** The Darwin Cordillera spans the entire region of the southern Andes and Tierra del Fuego. ***This page, top:*** In Seno Pia, we dodged a maze of ice en route to our anchorage. We saw evidence of receding glaciers at every turn.

Andes are not what they used to be. As in the Arctic, where diminishing ice is changing everything, ice in the Chilean canals is also retreating. Of the forty-eight glaciers in the Southern Patagonian Ice Field, all but two are rapidly shrinking. Runoff from those receding glaciers—the rivers and waterfalls that left us spellbound—is becoming an alluring prospect for dams and hydropower.

This pristine wilderness, unthinkably, is ripe for commerce. Even so, a writer jotting notes while rolling down the Beagle has an incredible opportunity to exercise nouns and adjectives. The channel was one long series of columns and spires, canyons and forests, fjords and inlets, snow and mist. It was raw, cold, and arresting.

High in the summits, fast-moving clouds skidded sideways in the big westerly air stream. The play of light and shadow was endlessly hypnotizing. Massive blue glaciers, one after another and each grander than the last, spilled into the sea. Way, way above, the panorama was a patchwork of blue sky, scudding gray piles of vapor foaming over the craggy landscape like a witch's brew boiling in a cauldron. The contrasts and textures—rock, trees, ice, and water—were spectacular.

Spiderwebs of waterfalls glistened in the sunlight, carving deep furrows of rivulets in the steeps. A huge cube of ice calved off a glacier and hit the sea with an enormous cannonball splash. Great piles of virgin snowfields glimmered like diamonds. It was a feast for the eyes, one course after another, and the courses didn't stop coming.

Fourteen hours under way, some 90 nautical miles down the track, we slid out of the channel and up a deep fjord called the Seno Pia. In an unsettling moment, the water's depths fell from 1,000 feet to 15 feet (305 m–5 m). But in another moment, we were back in deep water,

approaching a headland directly in front of us. We hooked a slight right up another, calmer inlet known as the East Arm, and then tucked behind a low spit into an anchorage called the Caleta Beaulieu. With a couple of tries, we got the anchor down and then ferried a pair of lines ashore where we secured them in the trees.

A trio of glaciers surrounded us. The whole place was spiritual, surreal, and sensational. Cape Horn had been incredible, but the Beagle Channel was a worthy encore.

FOLLOWING MAGELLAN

During the next few days, the long hours of motoring passed quickly, thanks to the fascinating terrain and waters. And each night we hunkered down in a private, majestic anchorage, oftentimes deploying the kayaks to take an inshore foray or to collect drifting glacier ice for cocktails. With Logan and Rockefeller swapping navigational duties, we wound our way out of the Beagle and northward through a series of canals and straits. As in Alaska, we were barely scratching the surface of this remarkable cruising ground; we came to realize one could spend a lifetime wandering these waters and never see it all.

Actually, sailors are discovering the Chilean canals in ever-increasing numbers; many spend several seasons exploring the seemingly infinite coves and bays. Luckily, as we closed in on the Strait of Magellan, through the word-of-mouth cruising network, we'd learned of a 16-nautical-mile shortcut to the channel that was officially forbidden to private vessels like *Ocean Watch* by the Chilean Armada. Rather than take the "official" route—which would've added nearly 100 nautical miles to the trip—we took a chance and pointed the bow into Canal Pedro.

A couple of hours later, we emerged undetected into Ferdinand Magellan's strait. The Portuguese explorer, sailing under the Spanish flag, discovered the waterway—which is 373 nautical miles long—in 1520 during his expedition in search of the quickest route from Europe to the so-called Spice Islands of the Far East. Magellan named both Tierra del Fuego ("Land of Fire," inspired by the many blazes he witnessed, set either by lightning or native's camps) and Patagonia. (He called the people there "Pathagoni," after the Spanish word *patacones*, or "dogs with great paws," a reference to the people's huge feet.)

Oddly, despite Magellan's self-absorption—which later played a role in his death in the Philippines—he did not name the channel for himself. Instead he called it the *Estrecho de Todos los Santos*, or the Strait of All Saints. It wasn't until 1531—six years after the lone surviving ship from Magellan's fleet of five returned to Spain to claim the first circumnavigation of the globe—that the strait was given the name by which it is known today.

By whatever name, Magellan's journey through the strait was arduous, and so was ours. The skipper's log entry for January 31 sums up one frustrating, if typical, day:

> *The log says we advanced our position 21 nautical miles in six hours. The last time we had those kinds of numbers, we were attempting to win the record for the slowest "rounding" of the coast of Brazil. We rounded a little island named Beware four times in our attempt to move 15 nautical miles forward to another bay—that would be twice forward and twice backward.*

FAREWELL FIFTIES

Once we successfully found shelter, we again settled in to wait for improved weather; the forecast wasn't promising. From our protected anchorage, we could gaze out into the strait, where a 30-to-40-knot westerly gale was strafing the waters.

On February 2, the rain ended, the gales subsided, and the sky cleared—at least in sporadic patches. The skipper basically said, "Enough." We also took a clue from the locals, regarding seabirds. When they aren't flying, locals say, it's time for boats and sailors to lay low, too. As we made our way back to sea, flocks of birds accompanied us, hovering overhead in frenetic flight. We took it as a solid, positive omen.

What started out so promising, however, didn't last long. Soon enough, another fierce westerly breeze came funneling down the strait, and we spent a long, difficult night engaged in a brutal struggle to negotiate a miserable stretch of water called the Paso del Mar. The old Yankee, Joshua Slocum, took a month to put the pass behind him on his famous circumnavigation more than a hundred years ago, spending weeks at a time cowering from the weather in an anchorage on its southern shores. We aboard *Ocean Watch* didn't wish to suffer a similar fate, but for a while, it looked as if we might.

Slamming into heavy wind and seas, and making less than 2 knots over the ground, we almost bailed out for an anchorage on Isla Emiliano Figueroa, but luckily, the onslaught diminished, and we were rewarded for our perseverance.

The big obstacle was a rocky island called Isla Tamar, and it took all night and a good chunk of the morning to get past it. When we finally rounded the corner of Tamar and set a course due north, the

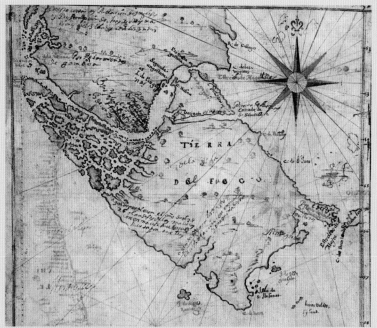

Opposite page, top: The view of the craggy Patagonian peaks has remained unchanged over time. *Above:* An early map depicts what Ferdinand Magellan called Tierra del Fuego, or "land of fire." Many European navigators followed in Magellan's wake. *Following page:* In a still cove, Herb McCormick enjoyed a reflective moment during a paddle in Patagonia.

skipper took a hard look at its formidable face, now receding in our wake, and said, "That's our second rounding of Cape Horn."

From there we passed through another wide body of water called Paso Tamar and finally cut back inside the protection of the channels, reaching northward up Canal Smyth and leaving Isla Manuel Rodriquez to port. We were finally, well and truly, out of the Strait of Magellan. Again, for perhaps the thousandth time, we were reminded of the skill and prowess of the explorers who first tackled the high latitudes, to the north and south, in engineless ships that wouldn't, couldn't, sail upwind.

At noon on February 3, the intermittent squalls stopped cold and the sun broke through in glorious style for the first time in eons. We squinted at each other like rescued coal miners. But twenty minutes later, the sky was thick and gray—almost bursting with ripe, low-hanging clouds on the vines of the heavens—and order was restored to the Chilean universe. By late afternoon, *Ocean Watch* was approaching the stretch of water that borders the Chilean national park called Parque Nacional Torres del Paine, a glacier-filled southern oasis for climbers, paddlers, hikers, and sightseers. As if in honor of the occasion, we rolled close abeam to a truly majestic waterfall, cascading from the steeps.

Finally notching significant miles again, we pressed on for the second straight day. As night fell and the sky cleared over several hours

of long twilight, the vistas opened, and we were treated to the finest weather and the best sightseeing since traversing the Beagle Channel. The solid rock walls and islands were one thing, but the most brilliant sights of all were the snowfields and the soaring ranges of the Southern Andes mountains, our first glimpse of them in the canals.

The fine weather continued through the evening, and we were able to keep making steady progress, despite the onset of night, thanks to working radar, wide channels, and skilled navigators. The rare light of the waning moon helped us find our way. By morning, the weather remained so still that at one point we stopped the boat and emptied our jerricans of diesel—35 gallons (132 l) in all—into the fuel tanks. Once that chore was behind us, we spent a long day snaking our way north through a complicated series of straits and canals, some with exotic handles: Collingswood, Sarmiento, Inocentes, Concepción, Wide. With the variety of waterways came a range of conditions, namely rain, fog, calms, and wind. Looking back at our travels prior to Cape Horn, we thought the Falklands had a changeable climate. By comparison, however, Chile was the absolute *Sybil* of weather, the land of multiple meteorological personalities.

We'd put another important waypoint astern. At 49°56' S, the furious fifties were behind us once and for all.

Clockwise from opposite page: Patagonia teems with life—including a breaching whale, flocks of birds, and basking seals—both above and below the waterline.

CHAPTER 14

A PRAYER FOR FRAGILE CHILE

On February 4, we pulled into the little settlement of Villa Puerto Edén, home to fewer than two hundred hearty souls; it was the first town of any sort we'd seen in a week. The tiny village immediately brought to our minds another fishing community we'd visited months before—a place that, interconnected entirely by boardwalk, had also been carved out of the rugged coast by sheer determination—the Alaskan outpost of Elfin Cove. We conducted our business quickly, filling *Ocean Watch*'s fuel tanks with two 50-gallon (189-l) drums of diesel—all that was available on short notice.

Because the next stretch of the northbound canal included a narrow, tide-swept strait that could be negotiated only on a fair tide, which wouldn't happen until 7:30 that evening, we had a bit of time to kill. So we strolled the narrow walkways, glanced at the meager shelves in the small *supermercados*, and bought a few small items.

During our stroll, we made the acquaintance of a gardener named Jose Navero Leiva. When it came to the topic of Puerto Edén, he was also a historian, and later that afternoon the skipper and Rosell engaged him in a long chat. His hometown's tale was not pretty. In his personal log, Schrader related some of what he'd learned:

> *Puerto Edén is a community of 160 with a school-age population of 14. The school is new and quite large, compared to the other buildings lining the waterfront. Streets don't exist; the town is perched on the side of a gently sloping hillside, and the sidewalk is actually a boardwalk partially cantilevered over an interesting shoreline. The jetty Ocean Watch used is relatively new, built for a ferry that stops twice a week, bringing to town everything from drums of fuel to fresh vegetables and mail. And there is a new hotel/hostel just across the bay, waiting for the influx of tourists from . . . well, that's the problem.*
>
> *According to Jose, the town is going through changes not dissimilar to those we encountered in the far north. Not long ago, residents here could support themselves by fishing and selling their catch to markets in cities connected to them by regular ferry service.*
>
> *They charged a fair price for a quality product, delivered fresh to happy customers in distant places. Commercial fish farms have changed all of that for the fishermen of Puerto Edén. Farms are producing and selling fish for less than it costs these fishermen to catch them. It seems no one is interested in buying more expensive, wild, freshly caught fish.*
>
> *In response to this economic change, the Chilean government decided to help with an infusion of dollars to make the place an*

Above: In Puerto Edén, we met Jose Navero Leiva, who painted a bleak picture of the town's prospects. *Opposite page:* During our brief stay there, we tied up at the new ferry wharf.

MAL TIEMPO

In Spanish, the word *tiempo* has two primary meanings: "weather" and "time." The world *mal*, however, has but one: "bad." With the exception of Rosell, none of us was fluent in Spanish, but on February 6, as we prepared to tackle an open body of water called the Golfo de Peñas that's renowned for its relentlessly foul disposition, we all noted—and understood—the repeated phrase on the downloaded weather report issued by the Chilean meteorological authorities.

"Mal tiempo. Mal tiempo. Mal tiempo."

They weren't talking about the time. Incredibly, the long-range forecast was worse, so we set forth on the 161-nautical-mile passage that stood between *Ocean Watch* and the next set of channels leading to Puerto Montt, knowing conditions would be marginal.

The considerable problem with the gulf and the roaring forties in the South Pacific is their geographical location and makeup. As noted, the westerly winds are tenacious and endless, but the Andes Mountain range extending up the coast makes them vicious and lethal.

Once the winds reach the long line of peaks, they have nowhere to go, no release for their powerful energy. Instead, they funnel and blow, stacking up tight stripes of isobars, lines of barometric pressure that parallel the continent. The end result of this confluence of wind and mountains is exponential.

Our first crack at the Golfo de Peñas did not go well; after an hour or two of little to no progress in massive headwinds, we turned tail and retreated to an anchorage to gather our wits and settle our stomachs. A few hours later, we made a second attempt, and got a bitter taste of what those isobars on a weather chart look and feel like in reality.

Maybe it was payback for our blessed run down the roaring forties along the east coast of South America. But it was a different story rolling up the forties on the continent's western side, and the long night transiting the bleak Golfo de Peñas was the worst single stretch of the entire voyage. It wasn't the 30-knot winds so much as the atrocious seaway. Logan said the waves had "holes" in them, and he was right. *Ocean Watch* fell into dozens of them, free-falling from the tip of a tall breaker into the deep trough with a shudder and a crash. It was awful. The skipper described it in his log the next day:

> On some passages we've compared the motion on board Ocean Watch to what being inside your home washing machine on the wash cycle might be like. I think it's an apt comparison.
>
> Only last night, we were in the industrial variety, known for its long cycles and vigorous turbulent action. If I were a pair of dirty coveralls, I'd be spotless now, ditto the whole crew. The spin and rinse parts were less fun than the wash cycle. It wasn't comfortable, but we're fine.

After putting the 60-nautical-mile gulf behind us, we still had another 100 to go in the exposed Pacific. Finally, we made our way back into the relative shelter of the channels via the waterway called Canal Darwin. The poor weather was mostly behind us, but *mal noticias*—bad news—was just ahead.

attractive tourist destination. The vistas are spectacular, hiking or kayaking vacation packages look interesting, sportfishing might be possible, but—and it's a big one—the cost of a ferry ticket for those tourists to enjoy the area is very, very expensive, the equivalent of U.S. $1,000 from the closest destinations.

The result has been predictable: No tourists are coming to visit or fill up the new hotel. That means no jobs for out-of-work fishermen. The young men and women, children of the fishermen, are moving away as soon as they are able; families follow if jobs can be found elsewhere. In three years the population of the town decreased by half. This is a community in transition—to what, they don't yet know.

From Puerto Edén, we sailed overnight to a deep, beautiful bay on Isla Merino Jarpa to rendezvous with a charter boat that had been dispatched to pick up Rockefeller, Treadway, and Cabot, who were due in Puerto Montt, which was still 400 nautical miles away. The inland route north, coupled with the nightmarish weather, had wreaked havoc with our schedule. Little did any of us know, the trio of newly minted "Cape Horners" left *Ocean Watch* in the nick of time.

WATERS IN PERIL

As *Ocean Watch* ranged northward, we noticed that, with ever-increasing frequency, the formerly empty inlets and coves were filled with enclosed, penned-in salmon farms, the "harvest" therein nourished with pellets of proteins and antibiotics that are causing pollution and infectious salmon anemia.

"The industry's solution (to these intensive production methods)—even as output falters—is to move south into pristine fjords, leaving behind waste, disease, and oxygen-depleted water," noted *National Geographic* writer Verlyn Klinkenborg in a story entitled "The Power of Patagonia" that coincidentally was featured in the current issue that we had aboard. "The steady movement southward by the salmon industry," wrote Klinkenborg, is "a source of economic opportunity and an environmental plague."

Remarkably, Chileans don't profit much from the salmon farms, which are largely owned by Norwegians. And as *National Geographic* pointed out, most of the water rights on the major rivers had also been sold to foreign corporations. Critics of potential dams that might be built in the future say they are redundant in a country with abundant renewable energy potential, and "running transmissions lines from these dams to Santiago will require a clear-cut more than 1,000 miles [1,609 km] long."

But it didn't stop there. Klinkenborg continued, noting that the abundance of seals and whales has disappeared, and that:

> Over the past century, the indigenous inhabitants have dwindled. A red tide plagues the mussels that once sustained the fishing

AS OCEAN WATCH RANGED NORTHWARD, WE NOTICED THAT, WITH INCREASING FREQUENCY, THE FORMERLY EMPTY INLETS AND COVES WERE FILLED WITH ENCLOSED, PENNED-IN SALMON FARMS.

economy. *The Alacaluf Indians, who once hunted and fished here, have dwindled to a handful of disconsolate souls in Puerto Edén, a place whose only Edenic quality is its distance from the rest of the world.*

But "the gravest danger to the Chilean fjords is, of course, climate change," concluded Klinkenborg, "which threatens to alter the rivers that depend on [the] glaciers and upset the balance of salt and fresh water in the inner fjords."

Those glaciers, of course, as we'd seen for ourselves, were endangered species in their own rights. And for all its remarkable beauty, we were realizing that fragile, gorgeous Chile could also be dauntingly at risk.

On February 9, *Ocean Watch* emerged from the canals into the fishing village of Quellón. Though there wasn't much to the place, after our trek through mostly wilderness since leaving Puerto Williams, it seemed like a metropolis. And once there, we learned that the fishing fleet had been ordered by maritime authorities to remain in harbor the previous week due to the severity of the wind and seas south of the city, precisely where *Ocean Watch* had been at the time. We felt some small consolation—even victory—knowing we shouldn't have been there, and that the weather had been decreed unfit for man or boat.

We were also told that the season's take for the salmon farms we'd seen had just been harvested, putting eight hundred folks out of work until September, six long months away.

ONE OCEAN, ONE ISLAND

We arrived in Puerto Montt, a true city of more than 150,000 inhabitants, early on the morning of February 10 after a quick trip from Quellón, a run of just more than 100 nautical miles conducted over still seas and under a brilliant, clear sky. After weeks, it seemed, of thick, stormy clouds, it was good to see that the stars still existed. The two main bodies of water leading to Puerto Montt—Golfo de Corcovado in the south, and Golfo de Ancud to the north, both to starboard of the big island called Isla Chiloé—were wide and dazzling, with a series of islands separating the pair that reminded our Pacific Northwest crew members of the San Juan Islands. On both rolling shorelines, the low landscape was dotted with farms and lined with sandy beaches—visual treats we hadn't seen in weeks.

Once boat chores had been addressed, during an open house aboard *Ocean Watch*, we met Dr. Cristina Rodriguez of the Chilean Department of Oceanography. Specifically, Rodriguez works for Mariscope Chilena, an arm of that organization that, in a joint program with the European Space Agency (ESA), uses satellites to manage marine resources. Included in these resources is the aquaculture development in the waters through which *Ocean Watch* had just sailed.

"South of Chiloé Island, where the Pacific Ocean meets one of the most beautiful areas of Chilean Patagonia, some microalgal cells grew and proliferated in the Gulfs of Ancud and Corcovado," Rodriguez wrote in a piece she coauthored for the *ESA Bulletin*. "Measurements in the sea could not reveal the extent but from space, satellite instruments detected how this population of microorganisms evolved." Earlier this decade, minute traces of these lethal organisms contaminated shellfish; hundreds of people fell ill and two died. The harvesting of shellfish in this vast reserve was shut down, and the waters declared a national disaster.

Since then, the tide, figuratively speaking, has turned. A big reason for cautious optimism is the satellite data that oceanographers have been able to use in such realms as fisheries management, marine habitats, and coastal-zone management. There was certainly a troubling dichotomy in the richness of these Patagonian waters, as the offshore yield had dwindled dramatically due to overfishing, but the area still offered "ideal conditions for salmon farming, to the point where the country became the world's top producer by the end of 2004." Rodriguez continued:

> Here, the coast of the South American continent is broken up into thousands of islands, which create a special environment . . . with a complex geomorphology. The ocean dynamics produce great environmental variability, enhanced by the strong influence of fresh water from heavy rainfalls and continental glaciers. The region has hydrographical and ecological peculiarities that are not well understood, but which determine the biological variability of its marine communities.

Clearly, there was much information to digest. The local waters were being influenced by internal and external factors. Powerful currents and upwelling existed from the roaring forties to the equator, greatly affecting sea-surface temperatures, oxygen concentrations, and nutrient influx,

Opposite page: Ocean Watch endured a thrashing while crossing the brutal Golfo de Peñas. *This page:* High seas and flying spray were frequent companions *(left and top)* on our continuing travels through the Chilean canals *(above)*.

all of which played important roles in aquaculture. But it was a tenuous interplay of countless variables, as we would soon discover firsthand from a phenomenon known as El Niño. Via satellite imagery, such data came to life in bold, vivid color. So, too, did algal blooms and rich concentrations of phytoplankton, busts and boons, in turn, to fisheries development.

It wasn't all doom and gloom, however. In fact, noted Rodriguez, satellite observations "of maximum phytoplankton activity in a zone where marine mammals such as the blue whale had been recently seen . . . was thus proposed as a new, protected marine ecosystem." And these emerging technologies had enabled researchers to identify dangerous and deadly bacterial species detected in the area for the first time, the origin of which was likely ballast water spilling into the sea from ships from foreign countries.

Rodriguez's passion for the ocean—along with her deep commitment to scientific research and her ongoing commitment not only to identify problems but also to seek solutions—struck a chord with us. So much of what we'd seen and learned in Chile had left us wanting to either throw up our hands in despair or kneel down and pray. But Rodriguez—like the scientists we'd met in the north—underscored the simplest of truths: Giving up is the last thing any of us should do.

And the longer our voyage continued, the more we came to realize that the basic premise on which it was launched was sound. A common strand did link everything. And while it was true that local challenges and threats to coastal environments differed from place to place, it was also apparent that the long-term effects and ramifications to people and communities were surprisingly similar. Whether it was algal blooms, overfishing, salmon farming, or the loss of sea ice, communities were being redefined, jobs were disappearing, young people were moving away in search of better opportunities, and long-nurtured traditions and ways of life were vanishing. From the Alaskan village of Shishmaref to the Chilean town of Puerto Edén, people were heading, in literal and figurative terms, for higher ground.

The Americas really were one giant island, surrounded by a vast, singular sea.

Rodriguez's ongoing work linking spiraling satellites with real-time ocean characteristics reconfirmed that most fundamental suggestion. From the blue sea to the blue sky; from the depths below to the heavens above; and from the tiniest creatures bobbing in the waves to the ponderous two-legged critters wandering down the shore: we are all in this together.

SO MUCH OF WHAT WE'D
SEEN AND LEARNED
IN CHILE HAD LEFT US
WANTING TO EITHER THROW
UP OUR HANDS IN DESPAIR
OR KNEEL DOWN AND PRAY.
BUT GIVING UP IS THE
LAST THING ANY OF US
SHOULD DO.

Opposite page: The image of runoff pollution from the city clouding the harbor wasn't easy to forget even though we arrived in Puerto Montt on a calm day in clear water *(this page, bottom right)*. In the Chilean city, we enjoyed many visitors *(top right)*, and teacher Roxanne Nanninga *(center right)* took our message to local schools.

CHAPTER 15

VALPO

Among the many cruising guides we'd referred to during our travels through Southern Chile was a handy book, *First Yachtsman's Navigator Guide to the Chilean Canals*, written by a retired Armada admiral, Alberto Mantellero. Mantellero lived directly on the shore of one of those canals, at a place called Puerto Elvira on the north end of Isla Chiloé. In his guide, while writing about his immediate home waters, he extended the following invitation to passing sailors: "If you see a flag on top, at the front of the hut, it means you are invited to have a sparkling gin and tonic."

As so often happens in the sailing world, Mantellero and I shared a mutual friend, a Santiago yachtsman and businessman named Mauricio Ojeda, with whom I'd sailed in Patagonia a number of years before. After setting out from Puerto Montt on February 13, by late afternoon we'd closed in on Puerto Elvira, where the cocktail flag on Mantellero's lawn was wafting in the light breeze.

Actually, he was expecting us, having visited the boat earlier in the week, when he extended an invitation to supper. As we dined with the seasoned seaman's family on steamed local mussels, baked salmon, homemade bread, and a selection of fine Chilean wines, we swapped tales of high-seas adventures—only a few of which were embellished—as sailors always do.

It was a superb evening, followed by an early wake-up call. As the skipper wrote, shortly after getting under way on Valentine's Day:

The tide runs at a fast clip through the Canal Chacao with the ebb flowing west, emptying into the Pacific Ocean, the highway connecting us to all points north, and eventually, home. At first light, we hoisted the anchor, pointed Ocean Watch west, and caught the fast morning tide. Very shortly, we were out of the canal and able to make our turn to the north, with a single-reefed main and full jib setting nicely on a broad reach. Blue skies, sparkling blue water, a pod of whales blowing and keeping pace with us just a short distance off of our starboard beam: what a great welcome into the Pacific.

The forecast for the 550-nautical-mile run to Valparaíso called for fast sailing before steady southerly winds, and perhaps even some unfathomable favorable current. It seemed almost too good to be true, but after what seemed like weeks of taking it on the chin, we were hopeful about its accuracy. Valparaíso is known by numerous names. Sailors of yore called it Little San Francisco or the Jewel by the Sea. Locals have shortened it to simply Valpo. The literal translation is "paradise valley." By whatever name, it sounded fine by us.

Above: Ocean Watch enjoyed a fast trip before fine southerlies on the voyage to Valparaíso. *Opposite page:* Once there, we were boarded by a very outgoing pirate.

160 ONE ISLAND, ONE OCEAN

EIGHT-KNOT HUM

Aboard *Ocean Watch*, when the boat was under full sail and really starting to roll, we didn't need to look at the instruments to know we'd hit 8 knots or more of boat speed. For precisely at that moment, the 64-foot (20-m) boat began humming. Months earlier, in the early stages of the voyage, Thoreson had noticed this regular, recurring trend, and he even gave it a name: "the 8-knot hum."

It's no coincidence that sailors "tune" a rig in the same way a musician tunes a guitar. As with the latter, one tunes a mast by applying tension to the "strings" of wire or rod that keep it upright, rigid, and in column. Sailors call such stays, shrouds, and supports the "standing rigging." A sailboat's "running rigging," the halyards and sheets, are the lines of rope that adjust the trim and set of the sails, both up and down (halyards), and in and out (sheets).

The source of the 8-knot hum was a bit hard to pinpoint. Our original theory was that it had something to do with the rig, or perhaps even the keel, but none of us were sure. Whatever the cause, *Ocean Watch* uncannily commenced to resonate right at 8 knots. As the speed increased, so did the volume. At 10 knots, it was good and loud; at 11, it really started to whine; and at 12 and above, it was so noisy you could practically feel it.

Hours after pointing our bow seaward, we were definitely feeling it.

As if to celebrate her return to her home waters, the blue Pacific Ocean, *Ocean Watch* was absolutely soaring up the coast of Chile in a steady 30-knot southerly breeze, and routinely registering speeds of 10 to 12 knots or better. As the day lengthened, so did the waves, lining up in long sets, and *Ocean Watch* caught her fair share of them, routinely surfing down the face of steep 10-foot (3-m) waves.

All too often, in our long sail around South America, we'd been bashing and crashing our way into similar wave trains, and it was exceedingly satisfying to run before them. Furthermore, at long last we were enjoying a positive boost of more than a knot of speed from the north-flowing Peru Current, a payback of sorts for the weeks of miserable adverse current we'd endured along the coast of Brazil. In our first twenty-four hours sailing out of Puerto Elvira, we knocked off more than 200 nautical miles, more than a third of the distance to Valpo. The rest of the voyage—during which we recorded 20,000 nautical miles on the ship's log and saw the seawater thermometer top 60° F (16° C) for the first time in many, many weeks—passed swiftly and uneventfully.

On the morning of February 17, with Valpo on the horizon, a tidy, 22-foot (7-m) sloop called *Polo Sur*, captained by a distinguished-looking gentleman and crewed by two young but clearly very able sailors, sidled

alongside *Ocean Watch*. It was Mauricio Ojeda, my former Chilean sailing mate, and two of his eighteen grandchildren, Martin and Sebastian. Ojeda had secured a berth for us in the same marina where he kept his boat, the smart little basin of the Club de Yates Higuerillas, in the resort village of Concón on the outskirts of downtown Valparaíso.

The yacht club's docks were lined with recreational sailboats and powerboats, which seemed odd at first; for weeks we'd tied up exclusively in working harbors full of fishing boats, freighters, and ferries. With our run of the club's hot showers, two pools, very fancy restaurant and bars, and Wi-Fi right on the boat, we felt like we'd landed in the lap of luxury. Once we were settled, Sailors for the Sea CEO and Executive Director Dan Pingaro joined us for a series of presentations, boat tours, and official visits.

But the highlight of our visit to Concón was the work of our onboard educator, Roxanne Nanninga, who conducted workshops on science and the sea with dozens of young students. Throngs of children wandered through *Ocean Watch* with their families and visited the crew during a series of open houses. We'd fretted about Chile's long-term prospects during our wanderings there, but the kids we met were smart, independent, and outgoing.

We were left with the impression that if those youngsters were any indication of what the future holds, Chile is in good hands.

OMINOUS EMAILS

On February 24, having taken on a load of fresh food and provisions— including a good stash of excellent Chilean wine—*Ocean Watch* set sail for the 1,300-nautical-mile journey to Lima, Peru.

On our second night at sea, as a glowing, three-quarters moon snuck up from the east, the sun dipped below the horizon to the west. Due to the dank days in Patagonia, it seemed as if it had been missing from our lives forever. The corridor of dancing reflective radiance glimmered on the wavelets like a trillion diamonds, like an absolute shining stream of lunar luminescence. We were sailing along the banks of Moon River.

Then another weird, wonderful thing happened. As the sky to the west grew darker, the stars overhead became brighter (sunrise that morning, off Chile, didn't occur until 8 AM). There was the Southern Cross, Orion's Belt, Sirius, and Betelgeuse; we hadn't seen those celestial wonders for a while either. As the bluish sky turned charcoal, the Milky Way materialized, too; it was a long slash of white across the wide, clear universe, as bold as the stripe down the back of a skunk.

The next night was just as enthralling. So the first seventy-two hours at sea were easy and relaxing, with perfect weather. Life was extremely good.

Then, in the wee hours of the last day of February, the reverie was broken. Though we were still off the coast of Chile, *Ocean Watch* was more than 100 nautical miles offshore, motor sailing calmly over placid seas. In the space of an hour, the in-box for our satellite-based email accounts was besieged with urgent queries: Were we still in Chile? Was everyone okay? Did *Ocean Watch* weather the tsunami?

The tsunami?

Opposite page: Fishermen plied the local waters near our berth at the Club de Yates Higuerillas. *This page:* In the resort village of Concón, *(top right)* we took on provisions *(center right)*. From *Ocean Watch*, we had a fine view of the lighthouse marking the breakwater *(bottom right)*. *Following pages:* The beaches in Valparaíso were bustling with sun worshippers on a fine summer day.

EDUCATION ON BOARD

Seattle's Pacific Science Center (PSC) was a cosupporter and the education partner for the Around the Americas expedition. Under the direction of president Bryce Seidl, the PSC developed a free K–8 science-driven teacher's curriculum guide covering topics ranging from ocean acidification to marine biodiversity. PSC educators Zeta Strickland, Sarah Bradshaw, and Roxanne Nanninga crewed aboard *Ocean Watch* and led education activities during port visits.

La única esperanza por el futuro de humanos y la vida de esta planeta es educación y la decisión colectiva para cuidar la tierra juntos.

Roxanne Nanninga

www.AroundTheAmericas.org

1–2) During dedicated classroom visits and at informal dockside sessions, the crew shared what they'd learned during their travels. 3) Hundreds of students toured *Ocean Watch*, including this class during the layover outside Los Angeles. 4) A quote from the Spanish-speaking Nanninga—"The only hope for the future of humanity and life on this planet is education and the collective decision to take care of the Earth together"—was part of a presentation at the Oregon Museum of Science and History. 5) The future of our oceans belongs to youngsters like this one.

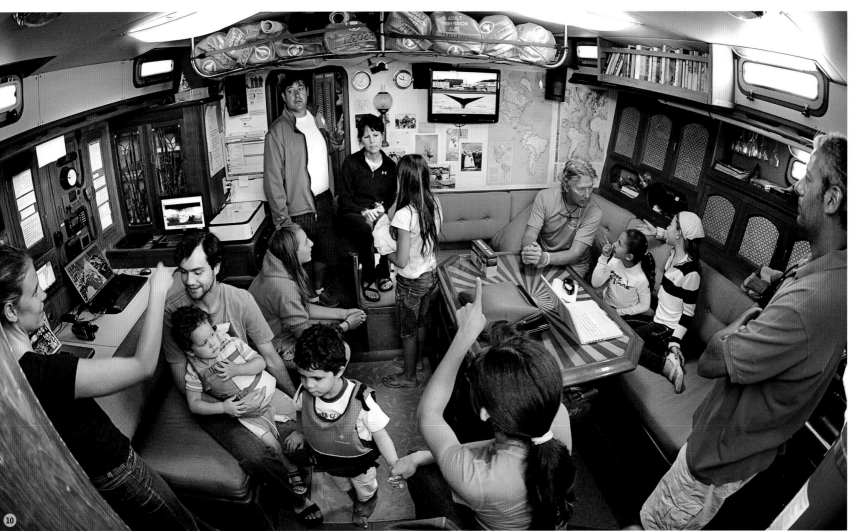

6) During the South American stretch of the voyage, PSC educator Roxanne Nanninga joined the crew for several legs and served as part of the advance team—arranging visits with school and scientific institutions—for others. 7) Whether posing for a photo with Peruvian students following an onboard tour, or making friends with a class of elementary-school students in Chile, Nanninga was an invaluable asset. 8) Pacific Science Center educator Zeta Strickland was part of the crew through the Northwest Passage, and afterward she demonstrated the Sea Perch underwater ROV (remotely operated vehicle) donated by the MIT Sea Grant program. 9) In Chile, students were quizzed on ocean issues. 10) Later, another group of youngsters investigated Ocean Watch's main cabin and navigation center.

SOARING WITH THE ALBATROSS

Once into the "roaring forties" south of latitude 40° S—and then continuing onward to Patagonia, Tierra del Fuego, and Cape Horn—majestic albatrosses were *Ocean Watch*'s near-constant companions. Writer Carl Safina has called these beautiful sea birds "the grandest living flying machines on Earth . . . wielding the longest wings in nature, up to 11.5 feet (3.5 meters)."

There are more than two dozen different species of albatrosses, all of which spend months and sometimes years crossing oceans, alighting on remote, largely uninhabited islands to breed before again returning to their natural element: the high seas. A parent albatross, notes writer Carl Safina, may fly some 10,000 miles (16,000 km) to deliver a single meal to a chick, and a 50-year-old albatross has amassed at least 3.7 million miles (6 million km) of flight, much of it gliding on thermals with taut wings.

Despite albatrosses' seemingly effortless flight and their ability to not only withstand but also revel in some of the harshest weather on the planet, in recent years albatross populations have been in decline in the high southern latitudes. They live on "thin margins," reports Carl Safina. "Working hard to wrest a living from the sea, they cannot amass enough energy to lay more than one egg in a breeding season." It takes a year for a royal albatross to raise a chick, and another year to molt and regain weight before breeding again.

In South America, albatrosses are in peril from fishing boats off the coasts of Argentina, Uruguay, and Brazil. In 1988, Australian conservation biologist Nigel Brothers first linked fishing boats with the albatross declines scientists were reporting, writes Safina. "The birds," he continues, "trail boats deploying longlines—up to 50 or so miles [80 km] long—with thousands of baited hooks. If hooked while trying to steal the bait before the line sinks, they drown."

PART 4

CLOSING
THE CIRCLE

CHAPTER 16

EARTHQUAKE, EL NIÑO, AND THE MISSING TRADE WINDS

The Nobel Prize–winning Chilean poet Pablo Neruda once said that his rich, haunting homeland "was invented by a poet." Perhaps, but that invention was built upon one of the most tectonically unstable regions on the planet, teetering along the endless western edge of the Southern Americas, with the high Andes Mountains to one side and the deep, blue Pacific Ocean to the other: literally between some rock and a wet place. Clearly, Neruda's poet was bent on anarchy.

As we learned via email within an hour after it happened, the 2010 Chilean earthquake occurred just south of Valparaíso at 3:34 AM on February 27, rating a magnitude of 8.8 on the moment magnitude scale. Afterward, the details came trickling in. A blackout that resulted from the quake affected 93 percent of the population and lasted several days in many locations. There were seven hundred fatalities. The resulting tsunami caused widespread damage to many coastal communities and swept away most of the boats anchored off the tiny island called Robinson Crusoe, the largest in Chile's Juan Fernández archipelago. Former President Michelle Bachelet immediately declared her nation in a "state of catastrophe."

Tsunamis race across the ocean floor with enormous force and energy, and the one that spun off the Chilean quake shot across the deep Pacific basin at an incredible speed. It's when those depths become shallow, along coastlines and islands, after all that undersea inertia reaches the end of the runway with nowhere left to go, that tsunamis become deadly. In Japan, the damage to the fisheries industry as a result of the ensuing wave was estimated in the tens of billions of dollars. Amazingly, though, only minor damage was sustained in San Diego, and most coastal areas and islands in the Pacific were spared. And at the surface of the vast ocean, hundreds of miles offshore, *Ocean Watch* sailed on safely and unwittingly. Had the emails not come pouring in, we wouldn't have learned about the earthquake until we reached shore. One of the first messages we received came from Dr. Cristina Rodriguez, the oceanographer we'd met in Puerto Montt. She wrote:

"The cities of Concepción and Santiago are much affected. Also many towns in the coast were highly damaged by the ocean waters and the tsunami in the Juan Fernández Islands. More than 147 people died. Puerto Montt is okay; we have food, gas, and water."

The news about Puerto Montt, where we'd made many friends, was encouraging. But there was one particular line in her note that made us shiver.

"In the following days the transport of goods to the south will be interrupted," she wrote, "as the country is cutted [sic] in two points along."

It seemed like an apt overview of what we'd experienced in our Chilean travels. On several fronts—and not only by the physical swath of north/south dissection in the aftermath of the quake, but also between the casualties and the survivors, the businessmen and the conservationists, and the cities and the wilderness—Chile, indeed, was "cut" along two points. Even before the catastrophic quake, when it came to the glaciers, fjords, and fast-running rivers in the otherworldly wilds of Patagonia, where commercial interests and environmental groups were increasingly at odds, Chile was a house divided. The quake gave shape to a concept we hadn't quite grasped: Chile needed to be made whole.

Soon we received another missive, from our friend Mauricio Ojeda, still in Concón, where many of the hillside homes were shaken from their foundations: "Ocean Watch was lucky to sail. We had troubles at the club. Although there was not a violent tsunami in our area, the sea [completely receded] after the earthquake, drying out the marina. Boats lay on the bottom, high and dry. When the sea slowly came back, the level reached [a point] much higher than normal [by 8 feet/2 m]. Most of the boats floated again, but three yachts were sunk. Piers were affected. But our problems at the club are only of material costs. No casualties."

Would the steel, 44-ton (39-t) Ocean Watch have picked herself up off the ocean floor and survived the grounding? We'll never know. But Ojeda was right about our "luck." In fact, luck had become a recurring theme of our voyage. We'd been graced by it in the Bering Strait; in our encounters with the Northwest Passage ice; southbound in the roaring forties; with the easterly at Cape Horn; and on numerous other occasions. As far as the quake was concerned, once again, the well of good fortune aboard Ocean Watch was overflowing.

PETULANT CHILD

Though we were stunned by the news from Chile, Ocean Watch continued making way for Lima. One of the best parts of the voyage was the continuous sighting of the elusive "green flash," the burst of emerald light that appears above a razor-sharp, cloudless horizon as the topmost sphere of the sun sets beyond it. The flash is actually the refraction of light—as in a prism—in the atmosphere. It's one thing to see it and another to actually capture the image, but our sharp-eyed photographer, Thoreson, did so on several occasions.

The fact that the still seas and calm winds were ideal conditions to witness the green flash were due to another natural occurrence—though one that was far-reaching and had much more impact—called El Niño. On the voyage north from Valpo, typically, we should've been enjoying fast sailing in consistent easterly trade winds. But the trades had vanished and the sea temperature was soaring, eventually reaching nearly 90° F (32° C). But 2010 was not a typical year in the Pacific, which was under the influence of a strong El Niño event.

In Spanish, the phrase El Niño is literally translated as "the Christ child" but in respect to both climate and meteorology it has come to mean something altogether different; the child that it refers to is petulant, ornery, and destructive. The Atlas of Pilot Charts for the South Pacific Ocean, published by the United States' National Geospatial-Intelligence Agency, has a very good summary of the phenomenon. Here are the basics of El Niño, as captured in that publication:

The term El Niño was originally used by fishermen along the coasts of Ecuador and Peru to refer to a warm ocean current

Top right and above right: Before and after scenes show the yacht club outside Valparaíso where Ocean Watch berthed before the 2010 Chilean earthquake. Shortly after the quake, the water drained from the marina, leaving boats high and dry. When it returned, the depth measured 8 feet (2 m) higher than normal, and several boats sank. *Above left:* Near our anchorage in Peru, naval cadets began each morning with a flag-raising ceremony.

Due to the nonexistent trade winds on the passage to Lima, *Ocean Watch* motored a lot. **Top:** This made fuel stops a constant necessity. **Above and center right:** Birds and turtles, our constant companions, kept the crew's attention. **Above right:** The dunes of San Lorenzo Island off the coast of Peru looked like a desert.

that typically appears around Christmas and lasts for several months. Fish are less abundant during these warm intervals, so fishermen often take a break to repair their equipment and spend time with their families.

In some years, however, the water is especially warm and the break in the fishing season persists into May or even June. Over the years, the term El Niño has come to be reserved for those exceptionally strong, warm intervals that not only disrupt the normal lives of fishermen but bring heavy rain.

Subtle changes in the interplay of wind and water in the tropical Pacific can affect local ecosystems and human lives in far-flung regions of the globe. El Niño can be responsible for changes in bird and marine life, coral reefs, floods, coastal erosion, drought, forest fires, and tropical storms.

thermostat for the planet, so the long-range effects of any given South American El Niño can be felt in far distant locales. We were already hearing from friends on the West Coast about the wet, severe winter weather—just one of the vast effects of the powerful El Niño episode.

PERUVIAN PIT STOP

Though we didn't have much wind, we did have company, including scores and scores of sea turtles basking in the sun. And very early on the morning of March 4, as we closed in on Lima, there were dolphins leaping, seabirds swooping, sea lions bobbing, and even a couple of small fishing boats plying the coastal waters. Disconcertingly, the one thing we couldn't see was Peru itself. Yes, it was visible on radar and on the chartplotter, but in the early haze and murk, the shape of the thing, the form and coastline, never quite materialized.

When the country finally did appear in midmorning, it wasn't at all what we expected. Before the mainland actually revealed itself, the island of San Lorenzo loomed into view. The southern flank was sandy, desolate, and utterly uninhabited.

We were only miles from one of the continent's major cities—Lima, home to eight million people—and even closer to our actual destination, the Yacht Club Peruano in the adjacent, working seaport of Callao, but we might as well have been on Mars.

"Welcome to Dubai," said Schrader.

"It looks like the Sahara," said photographer Thoreson.

The temperature matched the milieu. It had been a humid night, the decks damp with condensation, and the morning had been thick and hazy. But as San Lorenzo grew bold off to starboard, and the isle expanded in length and gained altitude—all bluffs and dunes, with a touch of Santa Fe–like striation—the sun broke through the milky sky, and the air became stifling and steamy. The fresh, open Pacific was behind us; now, just a little more than 700 nautical miles south of the equator, we'd returned to the South America of our travels the previous fall, of nuclear French Guiana and the searing bulge of Brazil.

Our stay in Callao and our wanderings through Lima were fascinating. People couldn't have been friendlier, and it was the least expensive place we'd visited. If it hadn't been for the beaches—littered with garbage from incoming freighters that dumped their trash into the sea rather than paying the established fees to offload it ashore—it might've been perfect.

But as we set out for the Galápagos Islands, we realized that the disturbing images of those awful shorelines were forever burnished in our mind's eyes.

In recent years, scientists and oceanographers have been able to identify an El Niño event with relative ease—the events occur, on average, every five to seven years—and 2009–2010 had already been described as a strong edition. In a global sense, what happens during an El Niño is deceptively easy to describe. The easterly trade winds along the equator disappear, the thermocline (the ocean layer that divides warm surface water from colder water beneath) along the South American coast plunges dramatically, and the nutrient-rich water from the depths fails to "upwell" to the surface. The consequences for Peruvian fishermen are severe, as the cycle deprives their catch of the food and nutrition necessary to thrive, and the fish disappear from the coast.

That's the short summary. But the weather dynamic at the equator, via worldwide wind and current flow, in many ways serves as a

Above: The crew never grew tired of the evening sky. *Opposite page:* Those sunsets accompanied by the rare "green flash" were particularly captivating.

IN DARWIN'S WAKE

Four days out of Peru, on March 19, the "advance team" of three swallowtail gulls arrived just before sunset, wafting aloft on the high thermals, well above *Ocean Watch*'s mast. The birds were like a trio of scouts atop a western mesa, taking the measure of a stagecoach snaking through the canyon. Once they had a bead on the situation, they disappeared, stealthily, to the west. They'd be back in a few hours, with reinforcements. They weren't after homesteaders, or even sailors; they were interested in smaller, more delectable prey. Those gulls were hungry for flying fish. They'd come to the right place.

Halfway between Lima and the Galápagos Islands, the crew was enjoying a beautiful day of sailing, making a steady 6 to 7 knots. It was a good thing, as everyone was working on little sleep. No one had wanted to miss a moment of the previous evening's show.

Given the circumstances, and our next port of call, it seemed appropriate that the Galápagos wildlife we'd soon encounter played the central role in the work of a young naturalist named Charles Darwin, who sailed to the isles in 1835 and began to formulate his theory of natural selection—the crux of his masterpiece, *On the Origin of the Species*—based on his observations there. Hours earlier, upon the first appearance of the voracious gulls, we'd witnessed a vivid demonstration of how food chains work, of the survival of the fittest.

The gulls had disappeared at dawn; where, we wondered, had they gone? After all, we were hundreds of miles from the nearest land. But that advance party overhead at twilight gave an inkling of what surprises the night ahead might hold for us.

The initial wave of the encore performance began around midnight, with birds weaving high overhead. At first, the fluttering flash of white could've been mistaken for a distant, falling star. But what we saw was much more immediate, and animated. It wasn't a galaxy of spearing meteors; it was a group of ravenous birds.

There was a distinct, civilized pattern to the subsequent banquet. Seagulls are not known for their manners, but the dining this night had decorum and very little squabbling. Food was plentiful enough to go around. The birds, several dozen strong, assembled in a wide circle, on a counterclockwise flight path. They would approach from ahead of *Ocean Watch*—never astern—and swoop in close aboard to starboard—never to port. There, in the waters abeam, illuminated by our green navigation light, the surface was roiled by countless flying fish.

The gulls would gracefully alight, pick up a snack, and flap off in a puff of air, without wasted motion. Not every pass was successful, but even on those rare, fishless forays, the birds would politely move on, rejoin the buffet line, and wait for their next turn.

Above: An iguana off our anchorage symbolized the Galápagos Islands; so, too, did the shipwreck we encountered on our approach to Academy Bay on Isla Santa Cruz *(opposite page).*

184   ONE ISLAND, ONE OCEAN

The one mystery to all this was the strange behavior of the flying fish, which displayed almost a willingness to accept their fate. In the light of day, they were zippy little creatures, skipping from wave to wave. But now they were flopping around like minnows grounded on an ebb tide. The display was almost too much to process: the clear reflections of the white birds on the dark water; their clattering voices, a satisfied, throaty purr; the frothing bow wave and gentle stern wake as *Ocean Watch* cleaved through the seas, each bright with glittering specks of bioluminescence; and finally, the radiant sky above, the ceiling to an amazing, dynamic auditorium.

At precisely 6 AM, the last gowned gull flew away, and the lights at the banquet hall were raised. You could call that final bird Cinderella, for it was surely leaving at the very end of the ball. Its departure seemed like a fitting segue to what awaited us.

ISLANDS IN TRANSITION

At the precise stroke of 4 PM on Sunday, March 21, the southernmost island in the Galápagos chain—Isla Española—rose out of the mist just off our starboard bow. It was a stirring sight and was perhaps quite similar to the one Darwin himself made 175 years earlier.

These days, the Galápagos Islands serve as the crossroads for international cruising sailors voyaging across the Pacific. This, in light of the chain's designation as a United Nations Educational, Scientific, and Cultural Organization (UNESCO) World Heritage site, an

Ecuadorian national park, and a biological marine reserve, have led the authorities to enforce rigorous customs and immigration procedures. So we stood off overnight to deal with officialdom first thing Monday morning. The Galápagos stopover was one we'd been aiming for with great anticipation, and it was fantastic to be on the very doorstep of this singular destination.

I'd visited the Galápagos for the first time more than fifteen years earlier and was struck by how rigorous the rules and regulations had been for private vessels. At the time, I'd been in charge of a group of sailors who had chartered two of the handful of boats available for such trips, and in two weeks of rambling about, we rarely saw another vessel. Back then, the restrictions on cruising sailors imposed by the Ecuadorian government were extreme, and it was a rare yachtsman indeed who was granted permission to wander about the Galápagos on his own boat. "Pristine," I remembered thinking. "This place is pristine."

It still was. But as we approached the lively harbor of Academy Bay on Isla Santa Cruz, another word came to mind: *busy*. It was very, very busy.

The very first thing we saw as we closed in on the bay was a big, three-masted "head boat" for live-aboard tourists that had come to grief on a reef just off the island's southern coast only a week before. Though ridiculously simplistic, it became difficult to dismiss the forlorn sight as a symbol of an archipelago in rapid commercial transition.

As we pulled into the bay, searching for a place to drop anchor in the crowded harbor, it was clear that it would take many a shipwrecked

Above: Watching ravenous swallowtail gulls feed on flying fish kept us mesmerized *(left)*, as did the sightings of leathery lizards on the Galápagos Islands *(right)*.

vessel to put any sort of dent in the charter business. At least a dozen large dive boats and small cruise ships dotted the anchorage, along with several dozen private yachts of all sizes and descriptions, including nearly thirty sailboats flying the banners of a Pacific rally sponsored by a British sailing magazine. To ferry the shore-side traffic into the adjacent town of Puerto Ayora, about ten water taxis zipped to and fro.

A stroll through downtown Puerto Ayora was equally jarring. The main drag and backstreets were lined with hotels, hostels, dive shops, T-shirt emporiums, jewelry stores, restaurants, and taverns. The assembled throng ranged from obviously upscale visitors on group tours to scruffy backpackers and surfers. Business appeared brisk.

Darwin wouldn't have recognized the place.

LEAPS AND BOUNDS

During the next several days, we met many people who shed light on the ever-evolving islands, particularly Stuart Banks, an oceanographer at the Charles Darwin Research Station in Puerto Ayora, who'd lived on the islands for nearly a decade. He confirmed that the population was growing by leaps and bounds.

"Fifty years ago there was hardly anybody here," he said. "In 1960, there were 4,000 people. Now we get between 140,000 and 160,000 tourists a year. In the last ten years, there's been an increase of 14 percent every year. It's one of the greatest increases anywhere, and that kind of pushes everything else."

Top, center, and above: In the Galápagos Islands, the amazing Charles Darwin Research Station provides an opportunity to visit with gargantuan tortoises.

Ocean Watch's onboard library included *The Diving Guide: Galápagos Islands* by Steve Rosenberg and Ellen Sarbone. Its figures were revealing. "Organized tourism to the Galápagos began in the late 1960s," they write. "The first live-aboard yacht, with accommodations for fifty-eight passengers, began cruising in 1970. A master plan for tourism written in 1974 initially allowed a yearly maximum of 12,000 visitors."

According to Banks, the influx of vacationers, particularly eco-tourists, was growing exponentially. But international visitors were only part of the influx. More Ecuadorians were arriving to benefit from the increasing opportunities.

"The majority of the present-day inhabitants moved to the islands from the Ecuadorian mainland since the 1950s," write Rosenberg and Sarbone. "Because the population was increasing so rapidly (300 to 400 percent between 1980 and 1995), the government had to do something to curb it. While the official population count was 17,000 in early 2003, the actual number was much higher (possibly up to 25,000) and growing, having tripled since the early 1980s. Legally, only official residents can work in the islands, where the major occupations are tourism, fishing, and farming."

Unofficially, we were told that there were upwards of almost 50,000 full-time residents at the time of our visit, spread throughout five of the group's nineteen islands—the rest are uninhabited—with the grand majority centered on Isla Santa Cruz. The trend was clear.

A lot of what Banks and other researchers at the Darwin center address in their daily work is "the inevitability of climate change" and how it relates to the incredible biodiversity that has defined the place for centuries. "In the Galápagos Islands," said Banks, "we still have the opportunity to do something, but that window of opportunity is rapidly closing because Galápagos, like most other parts of the world, is also developing very rapidly. Galápagos was once disconnected from other parts of the world because logistically [the islands] were particularly inhospitable places to be. Now all that's changing, and Galápagos has connectivity to the rest of the world that was never there before. A lot of our work is trying to assess the level of risk presented by this new kind of interaction of people in the archipelago.

"There are all these additional human effects," he continued. "Fishing, tourism, perhaps local pollution in port zones, local development, and how all that intersects with this complicated climate dynamic, is particularly difficult. In other parts of the world, people are trying to do the same, but there are few places like Galápagos, where in many senses it's a natural laboratory to follow processes and see what's really going on."

Thanks to Banks and his colleagues, the isles remain a living marine lab, and in that sense they are also a microcosm for the grander world in which they are a small but important part. Like the rest of the planet, more than even climate change or global warming, the greatest threat to the islands, and to mankind, seemed elemental: too many people. At least that was our supposition strolling down the bustling streets of Puerto Ayora, a tiny dot on a planet that might just be spinning out of control.

LONESOME GEORGE

Nearly everyone who visits the Galápagos makes a pilgrimage to the Charles Darwin Research Station to pay a visit to the gargantuan tortoises. After all, it's how the place got its name: the translation of *galápagos* is "giant turtles." The most famous, and stubborn, of these animals is known as Lonesome George, and he is perhaps the most confirmed bachelor ever. Now nearing his 150th birthday, George has yet to find a mate. Still, when one gazed into his eyes, he seemed like a wise, contented soul. And when you investigate the history of Galápagos tortoises, it's clear that he's lucky to be around.

In his detailed chronicle of the fall and rise of the isle's turtles, *Restoring the Tortoise Dynasty: The Decline and Recovery of the Galápagos Giant Tortoise*, author Godfrey Merlen travels back through the centuries before the arrival of men and ships, when "the archipelago remained a lost world where reptiles had become a dominant feature in the wild volcanic landscape." He went on,

> Above all, there was nothing to compare with the giant tortoises. Nothing could startle the eye nor catch the imagination more than the sight of thousands of these monstrous reptiles grazing in the pastures of the volcanoes. Their dark, almost black bodies moved hither and thither, reflecting the sun like water or glistening when wetted by the mists which swept through the orchid and moss-laden trees. Their colonization of the islands had been extremely successful.

> They not only succeeded in establishing themselves on dry, low islands, but on high, moist ones as well. Strong, curved, knife-like mouths allowed them to feed upon the spiny cactus and acacias when all other vegetation was dry and leafless through the lack of rain. Above all, their slow metabolic rate permitted them to beat the droughts that periodically smote the archipelago. Living at a low ebb in the shade of caves and rocky crevices, they remained like stones through months of blasting heat . . . When the rains finally came, the great animals eased out of their slumbers and rocky recesses and lumbered off to feast in a fresh and vitalized world, now leafy and green. Pools of water, caught in the baked land or on the sculptured rocks, awaited them.

> How many tortoises were there? No one knows, yet there is no doubt that there were many thousands—even hundreds of thousands. Some say a million.

And then they were gone.

On our ongoing travels, we'd been struck time after time by the havoc once wreaked by the worldwide whaling trade of the 1700s and 1800s. In the Galápagos Islands, the whalers struck again. The big, rich saddleback and dome-backed turtles were prized specimens to the crews of the whale ships. Easily taken, laden with delicious "sweet meat,"

Opposite page: The population growth in the isles is due to an increase in local Ecuadorian fisherman as well as tourists, seen here partying with locals on the busy streets of Puerto Ayora *(above)*.

and with a long shelf life, requiring neither food nor water, the giant turtles—which can weigh up to 500 pounds (227 kg) and live for more than a century—provided fine provisions for the far-ranging whalers.

In fact, the Galápagos Islands were a doubly enticing destination: Sperm whales were in abundance, and crews could stack their holds with hundreds of turtles for the long voyages ahead. A cargo of three hundred turtles or more was not unusual. In 1846 alone, there were 735 ships in the Pacific fleet. Aboard every one of them, there were dozens of hungry sailors. They all loved their turtle and took them by the tens of thousands. They loved them almost to extinction.

Later, it wasn't the men on the boats who endangered the turtles but what they'd brought with them and introduced to the islands: pigs,

dogs, donkeys, cattle, and goats. Some of these animals were predators, raiding nests in search of food; others were competitors for the sparse vegetation. For the tortoises, all of them were threats to their survival.

Ironically, the same creatures responsible for the devastation of the tortoises—human beings—ultimately came to their rescue, first in pursuit of scientific research, and later in the name of conservation and preservation. In 1964, the Charles Darwin Research Station was established, and in the years since, thousands of giant tortoises have been bred and/or raised at the center's captive breeding center and returned to their natural habitat. The turtles again frolicked.

HAMMERHEADS AND HANDHOLDS

The iguanas, blue-footed boobies, penguins, and seals are what most visitors long to see in the wild during their time in the Galápagos. To do so, one must enlist the services of a licensed guide. While several of the crew booked sanctioned trips to other islands for hikes and terrestrial tours, Thoreson and I opted to see what was happening below sea level.

The Galápagos have become one of the planet's premier diving destinations because, without fail, once you're in the water, you are guaranteed the opportunity to interact with big animals: graceful sea turtles; playful sea lions; and majestic rays, including mantas, that fly beneath the seas. Then there are fish—grunts, wrasses, snappers, idols, groupers, barracudas, parrotfish—of every size, color, and description.

Finally, there are sharks: white- and black-tipped reef sharks. Galápagos sharks. Hammerheads. On our first day of diving—initially

Top: The Galápagos Islands has become a busy place in recent years. Nearly everyone who visits snaps a photo of the tortoises. **Above:** The crowded harbor of Academy Bay surprised us. *Opposite page, top:* Oceanographer Stuart Banks has witnessed the recent changes firsthand. *Opposite page, bottom:* Luxury megayachts are chartered by well-heeled clients.

to a location called Isla Beagle on the southern flank of Isla Santiago, and then to a low, sandy island called Mosquera—we saw them all.

We also saw plenty of coral, in a variety of species, including prominent coral heads, intricate expanses of coral reefs, undulating sea fans, and big, oval sculptures of brain coral. Almost always, reef fish or sharks swam nearby, in various stages or acts of feeding or cleaning. It was a vivid, industrious, colorful, and vital panorama.

From oceanographer Banks, we'd learned that the coral we viewed was susceptible to changing climates and El Niño events. "When we get a strong El Niño it can drastically change the entire marine ecosystem," he said. "We've seen that already. We know that Galápagos corals are some of the most sensitive groups to climate change, and in the very intense 1982–1983 El Niño, Galápagos lost about 97 percent of its reef-forming corals in a year and a half. They were bleached through hot-water stress, where algae that forms in the corals is naturally expelled. It can always reintegrate back into the skeleton if conditions change, and the coral can recover. But when that stress is sustained for long periods, it's not possible. Then the coral starts to die."

The broader problem, of course, is that coral reefs are building blocks, even frameworks, for entire undersea communities. Banks said, "A whole host of other species—sea urchins, sea cucumbers, sea stars, reef fish—are all interactive and interdependent on this coral resource. So within about a year, the entire character of the ecosystem in Galápagos changed, because these are habitat-forming species, species that are particularly important in nursery areas; they give shelter and protection, but they also give kind of a three-dimensional complexity and structure in which other species can coexist."

Acts of nature were only one part of the potential problem. People, naturally, were the other. Overfishing also can topple the delicate balance in reef life. When lobsters and other reef fish were taken off the reef in abundance, the sea urchin population skyrocketed. "The sea urchin explosion infiltrated the reef structure and started breaking apart these reefs from the inside," said Banks. "In the past, people tended to look at conservation in terms of a particular species, like turtles or sharks, but you also need to understand the wider ecosystem function, and the interdependency, if you're actually going to make some kind of difference."

A second El Niño in the late 1990s caused more destruction to the reefs. "Today, coral reefs are fragmented across the entire archipelago," said Banks. "What we think has happened in the last ten years since the last strong El Niño event is that the natural capacity or resilience of the system to recover has been compromised. And only now is it starting to show some promising signs of recovery, after ten years."

We understood what Banks meant; the fragile state of coral reefs underscored the point we'd been trying to make. Everything, and everyone, was a piece of an important puzzle, dependent on one another—a cog in a wheel that did not stop turning.

On our final dive in the Galápagos, on a site called Gordon Rocks, where the current swept through a narrow pass at up to 7 knots, Thoreson and I underwent an experience "below the waves" unlike anything we'd ever seen or done before.

WITHOUT FAIL, ONCE YOU'RE IN THE WATER [IN THE GALÁPAGOS], YOU ARE GUARANTEED THE OPPORTUNITY TO INTERACT WITH BIG ANIMALS.

Following dive master Jimmy Pincay, we slipped off the dive boat and into a maelstrom. Descending along a sheer, vertical rock face blasted by what felt like 50-knot gusts, we picked our handholds carefully, knowing that if we slipped, the current would suck us into the void. It was like mountain climbing, but exactly the opposite. We weren't scrambling toward a summit but into the deep.

As we pulled ourselves down, hand over hand, our finned feet were splayed out behind us, fully horizontal, like cartoon characters in a cartoon hurricane. In what seemed like an hour but was probably ten minutes, we negotiated the first section of rock and wedged ourselves into a series of outcroppings. From there, we had a good view of what was happening in the pass. It was something to behold. Schools of undulating reef fish, as if a single organism, churned and pulsed past, followed by a flapping sea turtle seemingly on the razor's edge of control. A reef shark swam purposely past, followed by another.

It's hard to describe the sights and the sounds, the big sucking of air, the wafting bubbles. Every so often, a different surge of current swept past, almost pulling the masks off our faces. It was terrifying. And then, after a few minutes of it, after getting somewhat comfortable and realizing we were on top of it: man, it was cool.

In the final moments of the dive, before Pincay checked the air supplies and signaled for us to begin surfacing, and we made one last safety stop, we found another spot to bivouac and watched the undersea world go by. Neither Thoreson nor I ever knew how imposing a hammerhead shark could look until we saw one, up close and personal, and some 90 feet (27 m) down.

The Around the Americas expedition was conceived as a journey to spotlight the health of our oceans. Sometimes, ironically, we'd been so caught up in the concept, the science, and the mission that we'd forgotten about the sheer power and glory of Mother Ocean.

But wedged in those rocks, raked by those currents, surrounded by abundance—of color, of nature, of life—in a moment that was both serious and serene, we remembered the reason we had come here in the first place.

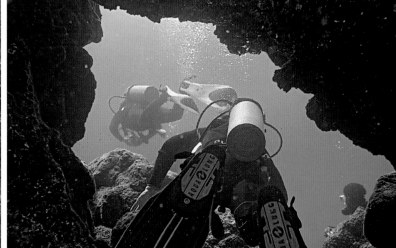

Clockwise from opposite page, bottom: Reef sharks and sea turtles are recurring images on a dive in the Galápagos. Colorful coral formations and portals abound. A dive master outlines the plan off a site called Gordon Rocks. Majestic rays soar through the seas.

CHAPTER 18

COSTA RICA AND THE BAJA BASH

We slipped over the equator for the second time on March 31, heading north a day after leaving the Galápagos Islands. We had aboard a pair of virgin Pollywogs—Bryce Seidl, the president and CEO of the Pacific Science Center, and Dan Clark, an engineer at the University of Washington's Applied Physics Laboratory who'd been responsible for installing and maintaining much of the scientific instrumentation on the boat—who had not yet been initiated into the order of King Neptune. Another new crew member, oceanographer Gretchen Hund Andrews, had previously "crossed the line" on a research vessel. As far as the initiation ceremony went, the rest of us found it more fun being an inductor than an inductee.

Early on April 2, Clark and Seidl made their first landfall as "seasoned" voyagers on the tiny, remote Costa Rican island of Cocos, a scuba diver's mecca and wildlife preserve more than 200 nautical miles off the Central American coastline. Most of us had never heard of Cocos until our visit to the Galápagos, where divers raved about the place. Since it was more or less directly on the route to our next scheduled port of call in Costa Rica—a marina and resort called Los Sueños, just south of Puntarenas—we took a slight delay to pay a visit.

It was well worth the detour. We later learned that Jacques Cousteau visited Cocos several times and called it "the most beautiful island in the world." It turned out he wasn't exaggerating.

Cocos is not by definition a big place, at least physically; it's roughly 2 miles by 3 miles (3 km by 5 km), but with a bit of elevation, rising several hundred feet.

At first, approaching from the south during a night of squally, unsettled weather—we'd heard thunder for the first time on the entire voyage—there wasn't a light to be seen except for the occasional flash of lightning to the far north. Every few seconds, there'd be another pulse of electricity, and the shadowy profile of the isle was illuminated and clearly visible, if only for an instant.

We'd stood off Cocos until dawn, and then, at 6 AM picked our way into the bay known as Chatham. There we moved into one of the half-dozen permanent moorings maintained by the park service. A big dive boat was on one of the other moorings, and before long a platoon of divers boarded a launch and took off for the day's first dive. Once we were secured, several of us dove in and immediately saw four or five white-tipped reef sharks hovering under the boat, slipping along the shallows. The depth was 60 feet (18 m), but the water was so clear that they looked as if they were 10 feet (3 m) away.

At midmorning, a small launch appeared and the park administrator, Victor Acuña, and volunteers Gabriela Diaz and Esmeralda Campos asked permission to come aboard *Ocean Watch*. They couldn't have been more welcoming.

Above: Skipper Mark Schrader pilots the dinghy on an excursion off Cocos Island. **Opposite page:** Seen from the summit of the remote isle, *Ocean Watch* and a dive boat are but specks on the water.

COUSTEAU WAS CORRECT

Diaz, who spoke excellent English, told us that from January to April, the busy season at Cocos, the protected park—a UNESCO World Heritage Site—received a lot of offshore traffic, sometimes a couple of boats a day. Anywhere from ten to fifteen rangers worked on the isle at any given time.

Most visitors are divers from the mainland tour companies or long-range sailors "following the trade winds," said Diaz. The latter come from all over the world and usually spend three or four days. Anyone is allowed to pick up one of the moorings, and if they're all taken, crews can anchor in the sandy patches. Though a small visitor's fee is compulsory (U.S. $25 per person), there's no restriction on the length of stays.

The only real problem—"And it's a huge one," said Diaz—are the fishermen who ignore the 12-mile [19-km] exclusionary zone and come in search of tuna, marlin, and gray-tipped reef sharks. "If you write about the island, please tell people not to fish here," she said.

We didn't waste a moment of our day on Cocos. When we finally left the mooring that evening to resume the passage, the skipper summed up our short visit in his log:

The superlatives describing the sea and bird life in some of our books really didn't come close to preparing us for how magnificent this little island really was. It is a diver's paradise, but birders and hikers would be just as satisfied with the incredible scenery and huge numbers of frigate birds, boobies, finches, and dozens of others species.

A few of us hiked to the highest point on the island while Logan and McCormick launched the kayaks and explored the surrounding bays. We all met again on Ocean Watch and regrouped for a snorkel along one of the bold-shore islands, and then we took a dinghy ride to the next bay to see a spectacular waterfall cascade from a high cliff to the shore.

We saw where Cousteau chiseled his name on a rock, dated 1987, a tradition followed by dozens of others, but they were all newbies compared to a barely readable "Martha, 1839" etched on a boulder near the shore. We didn't take time to add an Ocean Watch entry. We'll have to save that for another visit.

PURA VIDA

Costa Rica's motto consists of two simple words: *Pura vida*. Literally, it means "pure life"; in actual usage, the tidy phrase encompasses much broader ideals. *Pura vida*, in fact, is a way to live, an attitude to embrace, and a goal to aspire to. And from the moment we arrived on mainland Costa Rica on Easter Sunday, April 4, we learned that—for the most part—the hip, funny, progressive, peaceful, and environmentally aware Costa Ricans embrace the spirit of *Pura vida* as their creed.

The Pacific Science Center's Roxanne Nanninga, who'd sailed several of the South America legs as our onboard educator, was a fount of information about Costa Rica. As a student, she'd visited the country to learn more about its vast wildlife and natural wonders, and it was there that she met her future husband, Mario Gomez, a naturalist and guide who seemed to know every inch of his homeland. The couple led the advance team for our visit, and by the time *Ocean Watch* docked, they'd already made important contacts within the Costa Rican scientific and educational communities, who all understood our mission and message.

While Nanninga spent a busy week at schools and in labs interacting with students and scientists on behalf of our program, Thoreson, Clark, and I rented a car and hired Gomez to show us the sights. From the Pacific surfing mecca of Jaco on the Pacific coast, to the funky, Caribbean "Rasta" towns of Puerto Viejo and Cahuita on the Caribbean shore—with an overnight stop in the hectic, central capital city of San José—on our 620-mile (1,000-km) cross-country road trip, we discovered the pure essence of *Pura vida*.

The highlights of the trip were varied and fantastic: the molten lava spilling out of the extremely active Arenal Volcano, and the gorgeous lake at the foot of the mountain; the cappuccino and howler monkeys, some an arm's reach away, in the wonderful national park in Cahuita; the hummingbirds, sloths, sharks, crocs, iguanas, and butterflies; the high mountains and lush rainforest; the gorgeous seascapes; and the smiling kids—so many smiling kids.

There was only one problem, truly, but it was rather imposing.

BANANA REPUBLIC

The signs on the convoy of tractor-trailer trucks rolling up and down Route 36 on the Caribbean coast of Costa Rica were the first clue. Almost of all of them were adorned with one of three logos: "Dole," "Chiquita," or "Del Monte." Countless banana plantations lined the highway. We didn't make the connection until we slipped into the water for a snorkel on the coral reef off Playa Blanca ("White Beach") in Cahuita National Park.

For Thoreson and me, the rich and (mostly) healthy assortment of coral reefs and gardens we'd encountered in the Galápagos Islands were still fresh on our minds. What we encountered off Playa Blanca was not as pleasant.

The water was a milky blue following the previous day's heavy winds, so visibility was limited, but it made the snorkel even eerier than it might've been. Out of the murk, we'd happen upon a section of reef, and though some of the brain, star, and fire coral we saw was radiant and robust, the majority appeared bleached, damaged, or dying. You can't snorkel in the park without a guide; ours was a local fellow named Antonio, who'd been leading tourists to the reef for eight years. Once back in the boat, we asked him what was going on.

"Lots of things," he said, gesturing toward shore. "But mostly the banana plantations. They're just over there, behind those trees. They spray the plants with chemicals and pesticides, they get in the river and run off onto the reef . . ."

His voice trailed away. There wasn't anything else to say.

As we'd discovered at Miami's Rosenstiel School of Marine and Atmospheric Science, in the Spanish Virgin Islands, and in the Galápagos Islands, the world's vast coral reefs are in deep trouble on

Opposite page: While in Costa Rica, *Ocean Watch* anchored off a resort called Los Sueños, just south of Puntarenas. *This page:* On an inland tour, the crew was fascinated by the monkeys in Cahuita National Park *(top)*, by the extremely active Arenal Volcano *(center)*, and by the intricate and beautiful butterflies *(above)*.

countless fronts, and flourishing, vital reefs are crucial not only to healthy waters and sea life, but to a healthy planet as well. The state of the world's coral was also a primary concern of the Tiffany & Co. Foundation, one of the expedition's major corporate partners. In 2002, in order to raise awareness for coral reef conservation, Tiffany & Co. stopped selling coral, and the foundation continued to support research and conservation endeavors to protect corals and reef ecosystems, such as our circumnavigation of the Americas.

On the U.S. Geological Survey's Pacific Coral Reefs website, coral reefs were described as "the ocean equivalent of rain forests . . . unique ecosystems of plants, animals, and their associated geological framework [that are] home to 25 percent of all marine species." Like the rain forests in the Amazon and elsewhere, however, the living reefs are endangered. "It is estimated that many of the world's reefs will be destroyed or significantly damaged in the next twenty years," warned the U.S. Geological Survey.

Assaults on the reefs are twofold: Both man-made and natural causes can be hazardous to healthy reefs. The sort of bleaching we witnessed off Cahuita was largely the result of runoff pollution, but fierce Caribbean storms the previous two years had also taken a heavy toll. So, too, did warmer waters, heightened during our voyage by the prominent, ongoing El Niño event. Higher seawater temperatures make reproduction and regeneration difficult, exacerbating an already complicated situation. Overfishing, increased sedimentation, and nutrient overloading were other factors that caused reefs to bleach, a recent occurrence not only off Costa Rica but also off the entire Caribbean Sea.

SOLUTION OR PROBLEM?

In an Associated Press story that was forwarded to the boat with the ominous headline, "What If All Coral Reefs Die? Experts Are Scared," reporter Brian Skoloff wrote:

> Coral reefs are dying, and scientists and governments around the world are contemplating what will happen if they disappear altogether. The idea positively scares them.
>
> Coral reefs are part of the foundation of the ocean food chain. Nearly half the fish the world eats make their homes around them. Hundreds of millions of people worldwide—by some estimates, one billion across Asia alone—depend on them for their food and their livelihoods. If the reefs vanished, experts say, hunger, poverty, and political instability could ensue. . . .

Numerous studies predict coral reefs are headed for extinction worldwide, largely because of global warming, pollution, and coastal development, but also because of damage from bottom-dragging fishing boats and the international trade in jewelry and souvenirs made of coral. At least 19 percent of the world's coral reefs are already gone, including some 50 percent of those in the Caribbean.

Skoloff quoted Kent Carpenter, the director of a worldwide census of marine species, who said that if global warming continued unchecked, all corals could be extinct within a hundred years. "You could argue that a complete collapse of the marine ecosystem would be one of the consequences of losing corals," said Carpenter. "You're going to have a tremendous cascade effect for all life in the oceans."

After our visit to the reef, we asked Antonio for his thoughts about the damaged coral we'd seen.

"It's pretty simple," he said. "Fifty percent of the people are for the coral, and 50 percent are against it." In other words, roughly half the folks on the planet are aware and proactive about protecting coral reefs, and the other half couldn't care less. "Even the local people who should know better are out fishing on the coral [in prohibited areas]."

I was feeling slightly smug about being on the "right" half of the equation until Antonio added, "Even the tourists who wear too much sunscreen are damaging the reef." I thought about the big glob of SPF 30 I'd slathered on before jumping into the water, when a long-sleeved T-shirt would've done the job just as well. Clearly, even a guy off a boat called *Ocean Watch*—in search of solutions—could be part of the problem.

THE BIG BASH

When Schrader and Logan began looking for a vessel to circumnavigate the Americas, they found the hearty 64-foot (20-m) steel yacht *Danzante III* in La Paz, Mexico. Now, on April 16, after a five-day trip from Costa Rica, the renamed and overhauled *Ocean Watch* returned to Mexico for the first time since her purchase two years previously. In the interim, the rangy cutter had visited thirteen countries. Our stop in Acapulco wasn't on the original itinerary, but once again the windless El Niño conditions had reduced us to motoring for long periods, necessitating an unplanned fuel stop.

As sailors, we'd all become bored with the near-constant throb of the diesel engine since departing Peru. We were anxious for some wind. But as always, folks must be careful what they wish for.

When we set out on April 19 for Puerto Vallarta, our original and scheduled initial Mexican landfall, it wasn't long before the northwest breeze rose into the 20-knot range and kicked up a short, steep, uncomfortable seaway that made doing just about anything—sleeping, cooking, navigating—a considerable chore. Naturally, our course to Puerto Vallarta was directly northwest, and the wind, as sailors say, was right "on the nose." It was a nasty preview of what would be highly uncomfortable coming attractions.

We spent four days in Puerto Vallarta, arriving on April 21 and setting out again on April 25. Just a few hours into the leg to Cabo San Lucas, we came across a patch of white, roiling ocean that at first appeared to be bubbling like a boiling pan of water. It turned out to be several dozen porpoises, literally spinning out of the sea, whirling and corkscrewing with reckless abandon. We stared at them, transfixed, for quite some time. It was yet another sight we'd never seen before.

On April 27, we rolled into Cabo after another forty-eight hours of pounding into northerlies, but at least we had something positive and exciting to show for our pain. The ship's log read exactly 25,000—the number of nautical miles we'd traveled since leaving Seattle almost eleven months before.

Opposite page: The highway on the Caribbean coast of Costa Rica is lined with banana plantations. *This page, clockwise from above:* Only after we snorkeled over the bleached, damaged coral off Playa Blanca—the result of runoff pollution from the inland rivers—did we fully understand the impact of the plantations, whose signage we saw everywhere.

Leaving Cabo the next day, we had a pretty good idea of what lay ahead of us. After all, Schrader, Logan, and I had already made the passage north along the coast of Baja California two years earlier, shortly after the skipper had purchased the boat.

Yachtsmen even have a nickname for the roughly 800-nautical-mile passage from Cabo San Lucas to San Diego, which is almost always conducted in the prevailing north wind combined with a nasty northerly current: the Baja Bash.

Along the way, we knew of numerous fine bays and anchorages to tuck into and hide from the weather—wide, beautiful Magdalena Bay and the big island called Cedros were among them—but it appeared highly unlikely we'd have the opportunity to do so. A homecoming celebration, etched in stone, was scheduled in San Diego for May 4, and missing it, according to the skipper, wasn't an option.

The forecast was not in our favor. The clockwise breeze spinning off the well-established zone of North Pacific high pressure was mightily compressed along the Baja shoreline, which translated to rollicking northerlies—gusts up to 45 knots appeared in at least one forecast—funneling to the south. Once again, we were on a collision course with extreme elements.

Sometimes, we all agreed, life was very predictable. Our run up to "Mag Bay" was surprisingly benign, but as we continued north, not only did the wind increase, but also the temperatures began to plummet. We stashed the shorts and T-shirts again and went rummaging for our long underwear and heavy-duty foul-weather gear.

On April 30, having endured a forty-eight-hour thrashing, we collectively cried "Uncle!" and dropped the anchor off a remote Baja California village called San Juanico for a brief overnight break from the relentless northerlies. We were barely making headway and were desperate for a brief "pause for the cause."

We were under way again on May Day, and by 6 AM, seven hours after leaving San Juanico, the wind had fallen to almost nothing. As the day progressed, so did we, despite the filling northerly, which unfortunately again rose above 20 knots.

The next day we pulled into Turtle Bay just before 7 AM to take on fuel, where we encountered an anchorage full of northbound cruising boats that had been waiting out the northerly for several days. As we topped off the tanks, however, almost all of the vessels hauled their anchors and got underway. Clearly, the weather had turned for the better. Once we'd refueled, we joined the procession.

We endured one last bit of drama a day later when our propeller became tangled in a long length of discarded polypropylene line. Fortunately, one of the boats we'd seen in Turtle Bay, a 44-foot (13-m) catamaran called *Indigo*, responded to our radio call and lent us some diving gear, so before too long we'd cleared the fouled prop and were back up to cruising speed.

On the morning of May 4, in what seemed like a small miracle, a little more than six months after the Miami skyline had faded behind us, we were closing in on Tijuana, the border town just south of the golden state of California.

Clockwise from above: Running up the coast of Mexico, we met some unexpected visitors before taking in the coast of Cedros Island and the cliff divers of Acapulco. *Following pages:* We were pounded by relentless northerlies on this leg of the trip—hence the name of the route, the Baja Bash.

OLD GLORY

On our big spin around North, South, and Central America, we'd seen just about every sort of weather imaginable: storms, calms, snow, ice, and even a few waterspouts. The one noticeable exception had been pea-soup fog. Our trip up the coast of Mexico had been difficult and trying, so it was probably fitting that on May 4, at just a little after 5 AM, it descended on us like a thick blanket.

Fog, fog, fog.

Less than 50 nautical miles away was San Diego, the Southern California oasis we'd been longing to see for months. Getting there was becoming a problem. The northerly had reappeared with attitude the evening before. It had not been part of any forecast, and then, suddenly, it was upon us, one last bash—the final "south of the border" souvenir.

Then: fog.

We couldn't see North America anymore, but we could hear it. For months, the VHF radio had been mostly silent as we ranged up the coast of South America. It was quiet no more, and the traffic was mostly official: a series of Navy warships on maneuvers, and notices to mariners from U.S. Coast Guard operators in San Diego, Long Beach, and Santa Barbara.

Just south of the imperceptible line of demarcation between the United States and Mexico, the sky above began to break up, a patch of blue sky showed directly overhead, and closer to the horizon a series of alternating strips of haze and cloud appeared: blue and white, blue and white. All we needed to complete a patriotic scene was a splash of red, which we addressed immediately by unrolling the U.S. ensign on our transom, the big flag emblazoned with the stars and stripes.

Old Glory.

You can usually tell you've crossed the border by sea by the sight of Tijuana's big bullfighting stadium, but that was still smothered in vapor. However, just as telling and familiar, a battleship gray U.S. Navy patrol vessel hovered almost precisely on the invisible boundary.

Just before we reached it, we toasted Mexico farewell with a tumbler of tequila over ice, and then made our way across in the company of a couple motor yachts.

Appropriately, the skipper, without whom we never would have left the States in the first place, chose that moment to wander up to the foredeck so that he could take it all in from the bow. He was, therefore, the very first member of the *Ocean Watch* crew to make it over the border and home to the good old U.S.

After a brief stop at the customs dock on Shelter Island, we hoisted the main and sailed into San Diego Bay and right up to the pier at the San Diego Maritime Museum, the home of the famous *Star of India* and a fleet of classic yachts, powerboats, and submarines.

Above: As we motored into San Diego, it was good to once again see the Stars and Stripes. *Opposite page:* We encountered fog for the first time as we approached San Diego.

204   ONE ISLAND, ONE OCEAN

WELCOMING COMMITTEE

Among the many family, friends, and well wishers awaiting us at the Maritime Museum was a face we recognized—though we hadn't actually met the man before—towering above the rest of the crowd. Basketball legend Bill Walton, a native of San Diego, had learned about our expedition as we made our way up the coast of South America, and had been following it ever since. As much as anyone we'd met on our travels, he spoke knowledgeably and passionately about the utmost necessity of protecting our oceans, and it was an honor and privilege to talk about our adventures and show him *Ocean Watch*.

Along with *Star of India*, *Ocean Watch* was tied up near a couple of boats owned by another local hero, the four-time America's Cup winner, Dennis Conner. One of the boats was Conner's replica schooner of the original Cup winner, *The America*, and the other was *Stars and Stripes*, a sleek example of the latest evolution of racing yachts that competed for sailing's oldest prize. There was no doubt about it: We were back, and it was a wonderful reception. But it was also bittersweet.

Just two weeks earlier, the British Petroleum oil rig explosion in the Gulf of Mexico had unleashed one of history's all-time environmental catastrophes. The next morning, we read a story in the *New York Times* discussing the potential reach of the spill in the event of a hurricane, or if the spill drifted into the Gulf Stream. Once again, it struck the core of the message we'd been trying to convey: what happens in any one place ultimately affects us all.

Opposite page, top: Once *Ocean Watch* tied up, basketball great Bill Walton paid David Rockefeller Jr. and the crew a visit. *Opposite page, bottom:* The California coast was a welcome sight, with the beach at La Jolla Shores among California's prettiest. *This page:* California students visit *Ocean Watch* *(top)*. Appealing—but often crowded—beachfront properties line the state's long coast *(above)*.

The one silver lining to the very dark cloud was that, at least for the immediate future, exploratory drilling above the Arctic Circle, near Barrow, which had been scheduled to begin that summer, was put on hold. In the Gulf of Mexico's warm waters, according to some scientists, there was a fighting chance that the oil might dissipate. In the chilled Arctic, an oil spill of such magnitude could cause irreparable damage to the environment.

SPREADING THE WORD

Several weeks earlier, after crossing the equator a second time, the skipper jotted down some thoughts about what lay ahead:

We've returned to the hemisphere that holds the vast majority of the world's population. Our track will take us along the heavily populated coasts of Mexico, California, Oregon, and Washington. Remote places are behind us on this voyage. Our challenge now is to share with as large an audience as possible what we have learned about the fragile nature of everything we've seen, touched, and experienced, and to do so in a way that motivates greater numbers to respect and protect these extraordinary places. It begins with an appreciation of the vital role our ocean plays in everything we do. Ocean health is key to our health; no doubt in my mind about that, none whatsoever.

We now had a story to tell of where we'd been and what we'd seen, and as we resumed our voyage north, we shared our tales with and learned more from the scientists at the Scripps Institution of Oceanography and at the University of Southern California Wrigley Institute for Environmental Studies on Catalina Island.

In Marina del Rey, where we tied up at the California Yacht Club, some of the crew stayed aboard to host visits from eight Los Angeles inner-city schools, which included boat tours and classroom presentations, while the rest paid a visit to the Point Dume Marine Science Elementary School in Malibu.

"The 260 kids in this school welcomed us with a concert, a choir, a cheer, and a stack of ocean conservation 'books' they produced and assembled with their ideas of how to help heal the ocean," noted the skipper. "Point Dume has one of the most sophisticated marine science labs we've seen, anywhere. I wanted to enroll, but if you don't fit in the chairs, it's not an option."

On the move again, we sailed north to Santa Barbara and hosted an evening at the Santa Barbara Maritime Museum. Getting to Santa Barbara was simple. Leaving it was a different story.

CALIFORNIA'S CAPE HORN

In fact, *Ocean Watch* almost never made it out of Santa Barbara. Our planned ETD—estimated time of departure—was pushed back several days as steady 30-knot winds, with frequent gusts over 50 knots, raked the coastline of California. As sailors are wont to say, it was "blowing the dogs off the chains." From Santa Barbara Harbor, some 35 nautical miles

to the west, stood one of the last truly daunting obstacles on the final stretch of the voyage to Seattle. Point Conception has been called the Cape Horn of California because, like South America's Horn, it's difficult to negotiate and has caused its fair share of shipwrecks.

Still, by May 23, the skipper had waited long enough; we were going to push on to our next scheduled port of call in Monterey, come hell or high water. While we prepared to shove off at 2 AM, the weather forecast was less than encouraging; there was a high-wind advisory until 6 AM, and offshore buoy updates reported winds at 25 to 30 knots in various locations up and down the coast. Overhead, even in the enclosed marina, the flag was snapping in the breeze. However, we did have a plan B in place. The idea was to head as far as a little anchorage called Cojo just east of the point, and, once there, to reevaluate conditions. With this strategy in place, off we went.

The urgency was real; we were running late for a series of scheduled appearances at the Monterey History and Maritime Museum. For this reason, much of the crew who'd been signed on for the Santa Barbara–Monterey leg—including oceanographer Michael Reynolds, shore manager Bryan Reeves, and teacher Zeta Strickland—had already been dispatched north via car to wend their way up the Pacific Coast Highway to stand in for the boat and the rest of us. For the core crew of four, it signaled the first time we sailed as just a quartet on the entire Around the Americas expedition. We picked a divine trip to get to know one another a little better.

Motor sailing with a triple-reef main, we made pretty good time to Cojo, aided by a favorable current that was a double-edged sword; we enjoyed the extra knot and more of speed but not the seas that were stacked up due to the wind-against-current scenario. But we were making progress. At 10 AM, we were abeam of Point Conception, where we could see a sailboat high and dry on its shores—a casualty of the persistent winds that had pounded the coast. But we were doing okay, and the skipper decided to press onward.

So we carried on, noting the long series of offshore oil rigs, to seaward, and the dusty outline of the Santa Ynez Mountains rising from the shoreline. A couple of hours later, we were around the other significant waypoint of Point Arguello, dotted with buildings large and small at Vandenberg Air Force Base.

Once truly out into the open Pacific, however, the seaway became dismal. Though the winds had settled into the mid-20s, *Ocean Watch* was getting flicked around like a rambunctious child's bathtub toy in waves ranging anywhere from 5 feet to 15 feet (2 m–5 m).

At sunset, a wispy string of high clouds signaled the start of the windiest stretch of the day, with sustained winds over 30 knots, which gusted as high as 40. Dusk brought little visual relief; we'd been longing for nightfall so we at least wouldn't have to gaze at the turbulent seascape, but there was a big, bright three-quarter moon overhead, illuminating the wicked waves like a floodlight. It resembled opening night in hell.

To add insult to injury, the massive high-pressure system that had been in place for days had truly stalled to the west. Coupled with the stationary low parked over the Western states—the source of those compressed and funneled northerly winds strafing coastal California—it was sending frigid air our way. In fact, the 47° F (8° C) temperatures recorded that night in nearby San Francisco were a record low. Not only was it dreadful; it was freezing.

BY NATURE AND EVOLUTION, WE ARE SMART, ADAPTABLE CREATURES. BUT ... WE NEED TO BUY OUR PLANET, OUR KIDS, AND OURSELVES SOME TIME.

Opposite page: Point Conception is known as the Cape Horn of the California coast. *This page, top and above:* The seas along the California coast were often boisterous, and offshore oil rigs are a common sight.

Through all of this, amazingly, we had cell-phone coverage. And Thoreson, downloading weather from his iPhone, kept promising that if we could just hold on a little longer, things would calm down and smooth out.

And sometime after midnight—finally, wonderfully—that's what happened. Logan and I came on watch at 6 AM on May 24 to find a decided change to the weather. The breeze had indeed moderated and fallen into the 10-knot range, and, while the leftover waves were sloppy, the whitecaps had disappeared, and everything was in the midst of flattening out. And to starboard? Why, that was California.

Before long, we were making 7 to 8 easy knots of boat speed instead of 3 to 5 plodding ones and sailed abeam of the noble lighthouse marking Point Sur, one of the prettiest places in one of our prettiest states.

Monterey was just a few hours away.

HOT PINK FLAMINGOS

In the end, we kept our appointment at the Maritime Museum and also made a presentation at the Monterey Peninsula Yacht Club. But the most interesting part of our layover was a trip to the remarkable Monterey Bay Aquarium—and the guided tour, conducted by assistant exhibit developer Raúl Nava—of their latest, timely, and engrossing interactive show and display, entitled "Hot Pink Flamingos: Stories of Hope in a Changing Sea."

"The main goal is increasing awareness about the growing role of climate change on our oceans," Nava told us. "People don't realize that our oceans, 70 percent of our planet, are also being affected by climate change."

We were well aware, of course, that the very notion of climate change had become a highly charged, highly politicized national debate.

The flamingo exhibit—the highlight of which was the glassed room in which roamed a variety of scarlet and white ibis, Chilean flamencos, American bitterns, cattle egrets, and roseate spoonbills, with dramatic renderings of their futures should their habitats be altered—was but one small part of what was one of the more measured approaches to the climate-change issue imaginable.

With graphic displays augmented by video footage, the story of climate change—and, in a historical context, the natural forces that played a major role in Earth's evolution—was presented in clear, concise fashion. "For millions of years, the climate was changing," said Nava, "but two centuries ago, the industrial revolution changed everything."

That's because this is when we began burning fossil fuels and consuming energy at ever faster and faster rates. More carbon pollution began to appear in the atmosphere. Change is natural, but the natural changes are speeding up because of human pollution.

"It's the rapid change that's the serious threat," he continued, in one of the more enlightening and instructive statements we'd heard during our ongoing education.

"Wildlife and mankind have proven to be very adaptable. We need to act now to slow down the process. We need to cut carbon pollution and cut that rate of change. We need to allow the animals time to adapt."

The folks at the Monterey Bay Aquarium believe that when it comes to the topic of ocean acidification, there is "indisputable science" that the ocean's chemistry is changing quickly, something they demonstrated in the portion of the exhibit devoted to tropical corals. Ocean temperatures are also changing, but the greater threat to coral reefs is the rising acid in the sea as a result of increasing levels of carbon dioxide that have been deposited in the ocean as the years of burning fossil fuels continue to mount. As the oceans have become more acidic, structures composed of calcium carbonate (reefs, shellfish) are being robbed of a crucial building element (the carbonate).

Another fascinating display addressed sea turtles. After diving and snorkeling among them in the Galápagos and sailing through swarms of them in the South Pacific, we'd developed a certain affinity for the creatures. But we never knew that the warmth of the beaches in which they're hatched determined their sex. Warmer eggs become females; cooler eggs become males.

"So if beaches get too warm," said Nava, "scientists worry there could be too many females and not enough males to fertilize their eggs." "Hot Pink Flamingos" could've been alarming and disturbing, but it was anything but. Instead it offered suggestions about conserving energy at work and at home, and the underlying theme was one of hope.

But it held a greater message as well: By nature and evolution, we are smart, adaptable creatures. But we can't be rushed. Like flowers that bloom in the spring, like children finding their footing in this crazy, kooky world, the crucial ingredient is time. We need to buy our planet, our kids, and ourselves some time.

We just cannot afford to run out of it.

UNDER THE GOLDEN GATE

In late May 2008, almost exactly two years earlier, Schrader, Logan, and I had sailed the 64-foot (20-m) yacht *Danzante III*—the boat that would become *Ocean Watch*—under the Golden Gate Bridge and into the San Francisco Bay. The trip up from Mexico had been horrendous and revealed to us a litany of problems that would need to be addressed:

tired systems, bad plumbing, a lousy engine, and worn-out sails. The somewhat vague idea that we'd be back beneath the famous bridge in a couple of years' time after a circumnavigation of North and South America seemed not only optimistic but ludicrous.

And yet, at 1:30 PM on May 26, with jets of water soaring into the sky courtesy of the San Francisco Fire Department fireboat—aboard a well-tested, well-proven, overhauled, state-of-the-art expedition workboat that bore little resemblance to her previous incarnation—that's precisely what we did. Not long after, *Ocean Watch* was tied up at the San Francisco Marina in the heart of the city's Marina District, a stone's throw from the storied St. Francis Yacht Club, for a weeklong visit to arguably the most beautiful city in America.

Remarkably, considering our tendency to redefine the term "fashionably late"—we were never on time for anything, and the skipper enjoyed quoting an old sailing mate who had once observed that, "Sailboats have destinations, not ETAs"—we'd arrived not only on schedule but even a little early.

We'd left Monterey late the evening before with the core crew of four plus a pair of journalists from Seattle's ABC affiliate, KOMO-TV:

Opposite page: The California coast leg of the trip was marked by interesting conversations. The skipper met a rapt audience in Malibu, California. **This page, top right:** At the Monterey Bay Aquarium, Raúl Nava guided us through the "Hot Pink Flamingos" exhibit. **Bottom right:** Fabien Cousteau, with whom we talked in Northern California, is carrying forth with his family's work. **Above:** David Rockefeller Jr. addressed a gathering at Scripps Institution of Oceanography.

news and sportscaster Eric Johnson and cameraman Eric Jensen. While we had certainly encountered our fair share of reporters and members of the media during the last year, none had "gotten" our message like Johnson and Jensen.

Plus, they brought not only the tools of their trade but good luck, too. It had been a lousy, rainy, cold spring in Northern California—one last present from El Niño—and our final day in Monterey had been particularly nasty. But once under way, under the glow of a nearly full moon and a sweet westerly breeze, we'd enjoyed one of the best evenings of sailing in quite some time.

By dawn, the breeze had fizzled out, and we were once again motor sailing. But after the heinous voyage up from Santa Barbara to Monterey, no one was complaining about glassy seas and dying wind, and the calm served as a welcome respite. Aided by a northerly flowing current, the outline of the distinctive red bridge and the rolling hills and mountains of Marin County and the Tiburon peninsula—connected to the city center by the iconic span—emerged out of the mist in the late morning.

We actually had to wait a bit outside the bay, dodging crab pots all the while, to make our date with the fireboat.

The history of the Golden Gate Bridge is deep and legendary. The driving force behind the project was an engineer and poet named Joseph Strauss, who, though often credited as the father of the landmark, was in fact aided by a small army of politicians, architects, builders, and businessmen. Construction on the bridge, which ultimately cost more

than U.S. $35 million (but still came in $1.3 million under budget) began in January 1933 and was completed in April 1937. We were a day early for the seventy-third anniversary of its official opening. The Wikipedia entry on the bridge shared this anecdote:

> A graduate of the University of Cincinnati, [Strauss] had placed a brick from his alma mater's demolished McMicken Hall in the south anchorage before the concrete was poured. He innovated the use of movable safety netting beneath the construction site, which saved the lives of many otherwise-unprotected steelworkers. Of eleven men killed by falls during construction, ten were killed (when the bridge was near completion) when the net failed under the stress of a scaffold that had fallen. Nineteen others who were saved by the net under the course of construction became proud members of the (informal) Halfway to Hell Club.

Those gentlemen may have been halfway to hell, but aboard *Ocean Watch*, we were all the way back to San Francisco Bay. And we arrived in style, if we did say so ourselves.

Just outside the bridge, a zephyr of air materialized from the southwest, and we rolled into the city propelled by our big, asymmetric spinnaker, the one emblazoned with our unofficial but definitive logo, the continents of North and South America.

Once dockside, we took a deep, collective breath. It wasn't so long ago that getting back seemed impossible. But suddenly, in San Francisco, we realized we were a huge step closer to making it all the way back home.

Above: From *Ocean Watch*'s downtown berth, we could see the famous prison on Alcatraz Island in the distance. *Opposite page:* Sailing under San Francisco's Golden Gate Bridge was a major highlight and milestone of the trip.

CHAPTER 20

CLOSING THE CIRCLE

Memorial Day, May 31, which we observed in San Francisco, was also our anniversary day. Exactly a year earlier, *Ocean Watch* had set sail from Seattle. And although it was difficult to fathom, after this stop, we had just one more long leg back to the Emerald City.

The coldest winter of his life, Mark Twain supposedly observed, was the summer he'd spent in San Francisco. Now we understood. San Francisco may well be America's most beautiful, enchanting city—by a wide margin—but it is not a place for those of weak constitution, particularly if they're short on fleece.

Even so, we'd managed to have a full and productive stop, with a reception and speaking engagement at the St. Francis Yacht Club. Later, at a big dinner and open house at the Corinthian Yacht Club in Tiburon, we found ourselves in a roomful of fellow sailors, and for the presentation that followed we enjoyed the most enthusiastic crowd in all the shows we'd done since leaving Seattle more than a year ago.

Earlier that day, in a much more intimate setting aboard *Ocean Watch*, the crew had welcomed oceanographer and ocean activist Fabien Cousteau aboard. The grandson of the one-and-only Jacques Cousteau, Fabien Cousteau has continued to enrich and carry forth the family's legacy with his own projects.

After all the meetings, presentations, and parties, it was time to begin putting the finishing touches on ours. For sailors, one of the highlights of any visit to San Francisco is passing beneath the iconic Golden Gate Bridge. Inbound, a little more than a week before, we'd arrived on a sunny, deceptively gorgeous afternoon (the temperatures started diving the instant the bridge was overhead). However, when we edged around the breakwater from our berth at the San Francisco municipal marina at 6 AM on June 5 to make our outbound journey into the Pacific Ocean and on to Portland, Oregon, we were engulfed in a thick, enveloping blanket of dense, gray fog.

During our layover, we'd passed by the famous Fog City Diner. Now we knew the derivation of its name.

We could *hear* the bridge—its bells and sirens—a good while before we could *see* it. Tucked behind the inner steering station, with one hand on the helm and both eyes on the radar screen, Logan did a masterful job piloting us through the incoming shipping traffic, and we were almost directly beneath the Golden Gate's wide, red center span before its form suddenly materialized out of the mist. We craned our necks skyward for a fleeting glimpse—and then, presto!—the entire structure vanished. You don't need David Copperfield's magical powers to pull off a disappearing act on a dramatic San Francisco morning.

Above: Once we'd reached Portland, Oregon, the voyage was nearing its completion. *Opposite page:* Outbound over the Columbia River Bar, we learned firsthand about its hazards and reputation.

214   ONE ISLAND, ONE OCEAN

CROSSING THE BAR

Metaphorically, a mariner is said to "cross the bar" and sail on to "Fiddler's Green" when his days on this watery world have come to a close and he's made his final passage. Aboard *Ocean Watch*, we were all alive and well, but on June 8 we indeed crossed a bar, the notorious one at the mouth of the Columbia River.

For two days, we'd marveled at the glorious sailing conditions, but the night before we reached the river, we were belted by a nagging northerly breeze and topsy-turvy seas that provided a good twelve to thirteen hours of carnival-ride thrills. Happily, after a radiant dawn light show that began at the stroke of 4 AM and continued for the next couple of hours—in length and hue, it was reminiscent of an Arctic daybreak— the winds and seas both began to settle down. After crunching into progress-killing head seas for much of the long night, sometimes cutting boat speed to 3 to 4 knots, the calming conditions allowed us to resume speeds over 7 knots. Once more, *Ocean Watch* was a going concern.

Closing in on the stark coast of Oregon, we again had a good view of the West Coast, which in many places was a patchwork of green not unlike an emerald quilt. The dark bits, as it turned out, were forest, the light ones large expanses where forest used to exist. "We're back in the Pacific Northwest," said Logan, ruefully. "Look at all those clear-cuts. So bizarre."

As we closed in on the Columbia, the skipper addressed the local hazards and attractions in his personal log:

Our trusty Coast Pilot Sailing Directions *notes the following: "The Columbia River bar is reported to be very dangerous*

because of sudden and unpredictable changes in the currents often accompanied by large breakers." We've seen the pictures of Coast Guard rescue boats and other commercial craft getting rolled while coming or going across the bar when conditions weren't favorable. If the currents weren't so fierce, I'm guessing the salvage diving would be pretty fantastic.

Our plan for the bar crossing is a cautious one. We'll make our approach and stand just offshore until the tide is slack, going to flood, and then we'll "ride" that tide into Astoria and stay for the night. The trip up the Columbia will take all of our daylight hours tomorrow. It is approximately 90 [nautical] miles of scenic, curving waterway with current against us most of the way because of recent heavy rains and flooding. If all goes well, tomorrow night will find Ocean Watch and crew safely moored in downtown Portland: sailors in the big city one last time before heading home.

On our final approach, Logan pointed out the once-mighty Mount St. Helens, or what remains of it. "It's the one with the top blown off," he noted, helpfully. "Over here is Oregon; over there is Washington," he said, pointing at the coastline. "We're headed for that low space in the middle."

That was the Columbia River. At 4:30 PM local time, we were a couple miles away, so Logan called the river pilots on the VHF radio and was told seas were running 3 feet to 5 feet (1 m–2 m) in the pass, and there were no traffic restrictions.

"We're going in," he said. It was a cool, gray afternoon, but once in the channel, the swells were considerably less than 5 feet (2 m). There was

AS AT CAPE HORN,
THE EMOTION HERE
CAUGHT US BY
SURPRISE. WHEN
WE MOTORED INTO
THE LITTLE FISHING
VILLAGE OF NEAH
BAY ... WE COULDN'T
HAVE BEEN HAPPIER.

Opposite page: Slamming up the coast of Washington, we experienced one last "nosebleed." *This page, top:* The lighthouse on Tatoosh Island signaled the end of our Pacific voyaging. *Above:* Once in calm waters, the sun shone on *Ocean Watch*'s core crew (from left): Michael Reynolds, Mark Schrader, David Thoreson, Dave Logan, and Herb McCormick.

a slight heave to the glassy seas once we'd entered the channel, where the depth dropped from well over 100 feet (30 m) to just over 50 feet (15 m), but conditions were benign.

"I've never seen it this flat, at sea or ashore," said Logan. "This is amazing. If we were here two days ago, we'd be upside down by now. I've been to this bar twenty-five times, both by land and sea, and I've never seen it like this before."

A couple of hours later, we'd well and truly crossed the bar and were tied up in Astoria on familiar, Pacific Northwest turf. "Fir trees," said Logan. "I haven't seen those in a long time."

AROUND THE CORNER

Sandwiched around our open house and speaking engagement at the Oregon Museum of Science and Industry in the heart of downtown Portland, our runs up and down the lovely Columbia River were interesting and gleefully uneventful, with a host of guests that we picked up and dropped off at Astoria.

Then, on June 12, with scientists Michael Reynolds (who'd sailed most of the voyage alongside our core team) and Axel Schweiger, and our beloved sailmaker, Carol Hasse—whose loft, Port Townsend Sails, had crafted the bulk of our beautiful, bulletproof sails—we began the final leg of our voyage, back to Seattle.

Given the winds hovering near 20 knots and 5-foot to 7-foot (1-m to 2-m) waves, our second, outbound crossing of the bar proved to be more daunting than our inbound transit. And that night, our final one offshore, was a stomach-tossing experience in yet another annoying northerly. Thoreson had come up with a pithy description of these endlessly miserable experiences: nosebleeds.

But that was the end of them. We'd seen our fair share of capes and points on the circumnavigation of the Americas: At the apex of North America we gazed upon a glorified sand spit called Zenith Point, and at the very end of South America we took in true glory in all its wild majesty at the grand and legendary Cape Horn.

Along the Eastern Seaboard alone, we negotiated Cape Cod, Cape May, Cape Hatteras, Cape Lookout, and Cape Canaveral. It took us forever to get past Punta Calcanhar on the east coast of Brazil, and on the other side of the continents, we got creamed soon after losing sight of, first, Cabo San Lucas, and later, Point Conception.

But on June 14, we rounded perhaps the most momentous of them all, Cape Flattery, in Washington. That's because it was the last one.

It wasn't easy. The lighthouse at Tatoosh Island is actually the landmark off the cape that needs to be negotiated before turning the corner out of the Pacific and into Neah Bay.

In the miles leading up to it, though it was a gray day, the coastline was beautiful, and Hasse, in her home waters, described much of the history and geography. The first American to circumnavigate, Captain Robert Gray, was a Bostonian fur trader; he named both the Columbia River and, a little farther north, Gray's Harbor.

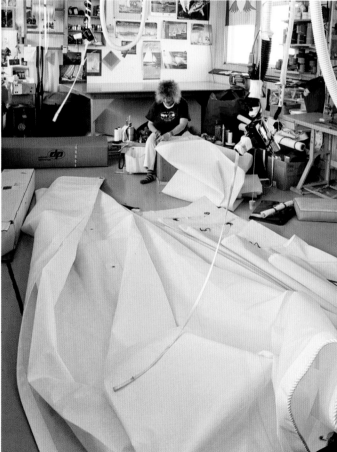

As we sailed on, Hasse pointed out the sea stacks known as the Needles, and Cape Alava along the rustic coast of Olympic National Park's wilderness beach. If it had been a clear day, she said, we would've seen Mount Olympus, the rain forest that receives more moisture each year than any place else in the continental United States, which of course is why we couldn't see it.

And then, finally, there was Cape Flattery and the lighthouse on Tatoosh, the home of the Makah Nation, the great Native American whalers and craftsmen of the Pacific Northwest.

The "Corner." We were at the corner.

As at Cape Horn, the emotions we experienced upon arriving here were stronger than we expected and caught us by surprise. We took a hundred pictures. We hugged and laughed.

And then, we turned the boat, dropped the sails, and motored into the little fishing village of Neah Bay.

It was quite cold. We were tired, and all in desperate need of hot showers, pounds of soap, and vats of shampoo. Still, we could not have been happier.

Opposite page, left and center: Sailmaker Carol Hasse accompanied us on the journey's final leg. Her team at Port Townsend Sails built *Ocean Watch*'s bulletproof sail inventory. *This page, top left:* In Port Townsend, David Rockefeller Jr. uses a slide presentation to describe our voyage. *Top right and above:* The port, which is a wooden boat mecca, gave us a wonderful reception. *Following pages:* In Seattle, we were escorted home by one last fireboat.

A CIRCLE CLOSED

There was just one more stop to make. When we left Seattle a little more than a year earlier, our first call was at Port Townsend, so it made sense to check in on the way back. The next night, Hasse's mates and coworkers and our friends in the lovely Victorian village threw us a bash at the Northwest Maritime Center and Wooden Boat Foundation that we'd never forget.

Then, on June 17, we set a course for Seattle.

For the final miles down Puget Sound from Port Townsend, the core crew was joined by a boatload of scientists, supporters, sponsors, and friends who'd played a major role in the journey and logged significant miles on different legs of the voyage. The day started early, at a shade past 5 AM, and by the time Shilshole Bay Marina hove into view, a fine spectator fleet had joined *Ocean Watch* to welcome her home.

After 382 incredible days and with 25,524 nautical miles in her wake, the 64-foot (20-m) cutter slipped behind the breakwater at Shilshole, back where it started. What began as a dream, and not a particularly reasonable one, concluded with streams of water aimed skyward from the hoses of a Seattle Fire Department rescue tug. As the mist from the fireboat settled back into the sea, kids on the beach waved signs and greetings, and a throng of people lined the docks as Logan nestled the steel yacht alongside for the final time. To the crowd, the skipper said, "It's a magnificent highway out there, and we took it."

Several years earlier, on a voyage with his mates David Rockefeller Jr. and David Treadway, the conversation turned to the topic of ocean health and changing climates, and before too long, Schrader was again searching for his pencil, just as he had when he was a kid in Nebraska and something piqued his interest. Whether it was a cornfield or a neighbor's farm, to get a sense of the place, to define its parameters, he drew a circle around it. What he doodled this time was a large loop on a map of North and South America, and the trip it symbolized was something altogether different than a lap around low, flat Midwest terrain.

No, the idea this time was to set sail on what might best be described as an environmental adventure, a long voyage of learning, research, awareness, and discovery on a relatively tiny boat. The journey would dramatize and symbolize the notion that the American continents were a single island surrounded by a common ocean; that what happened on the land would ultimately affect the watery world that surrounded it; and that it was in the best interests of all of us to protect and conserve this most precious, life-sustaining resource.

The circle on the map would ultimately be known as the Around the Americas expedition, and it would come to consume the dreams and lives of not only the three chaps who conceived it, but also a wide team of sailors, scientists, teachers, and students, as well as countless citizens of that great big island of all ages, from all walks of life. That circle became an odyssey, an adventure, and a quest.

And it finished on a surprising note. We set out to try, in some very small way, to help change the world, and we ended up changing ourselves.

It was hard to believe, but it was true. The circle around the Americas was closed.

Clockwise from this page, top left: Once back in Seattle, the celebration began in earnest. Students who'd followed the voyage paid a visit to *Ocean Watch*. Thoreson and McCormick shared an embrace. Many of the scientists and supporters who sailed the last leg from Port Townsend waved to the shore-side greeters. Skipper Schrader flashed a thumb's up with exhibition supporters Bryce Seidl (left) and David Rockefeller Jr. Schrader and Sailors for the Sea cofounder David Treadway posed with some young sign bearers. Having closed the circle around the Americas, the captain was all smiles.

WELCOME HOME OCEAN WATCH

PLASTIC POLLUTION AND
THE PACIFIC GARBAGE PATCH

The great Pacific "garbage patch" is another term for the so-called "trash vortex" formed by a series of interconnected ocean currents in the North Pacific Gyre. One of the misconceptions about the Pacific garbage patch is that it's a giant, swirling island of trash. It's more like a vast cauldron of synthetic stew composed of high concentrations of plastic in the eastern and western Pacific, respectively.

1) Toxic additives used to manufacture plastic items can leach out into their surroundings when exposed to water. And because waterborne hydrophobic pollutants collect and magnify on the surface of plastic trash, the plastic itself is far more deadly in the ocean than on land. The effects of ultraviolet radiation, and wind and wave action, break plastic goods into ever-smaller individual shards, called *microplastics*, which are ingested by fish and spread through the food chain. Though *Ocean Watch* did not venture offshore in the North Pacific, the crew witnessed plastic pollutants on countless occasions. Near Lima, Peru, the carcasses of dead birds that had ingested plastic were a sobering sight. 2) Many freighters deposit their litter offshore to avoid harbor fees for its removal; the garbage eventually drifts ashore. 3) Farther north, off Central America, the crew cut away discarded synthetic fishing nets that became wrapped around the keel. 4) Even in progressive Portland, Oregon, we encountered a plastic mess during a paddle off the Columbia River.

5) "The crab photo is just one of many I took at the 'plastic beach' near Lima," said photographer David Thoreson. "I wanted to zoom in to show the smaller dead organic species like the crab mixed in among the plastics (yes, the yellow thing is plastic, too). The beach made me nauseous as it reeked of dead, decaying organic matter." 6) In San Francisco, conservationist Manuel Maqueda of the Plastics Pollution Coalition said, "In the United States alone, every week, we discard 500 million plastic bottles for water, enough to go around the planet five times." 7) Dr. Marcus Eriksen and his wife, Anna Cummins, are pioneers in the study of ocean gyres and plastics accumulation. Their organization, 5 Gyres, is named after the planet's five major circulating currents. The group's mission is to research and expose the global impact of plastic pollution, which is a threat to oceans and sea life all over the planet, not just in the North Pacific. 8) A plastic bottle drifting in dirty seawater in the mostly pristine Falkland Islands underscored that fact. 9) The Gulf Stream, which warms Western Europe, is part of a network of ocean currents driven by warm tropical water. These powerful currents can transport pollutants vast distances. However, some scientists fear global warming will weaken these currents, causing the tropics to overheat and northern continents to become even cooler.

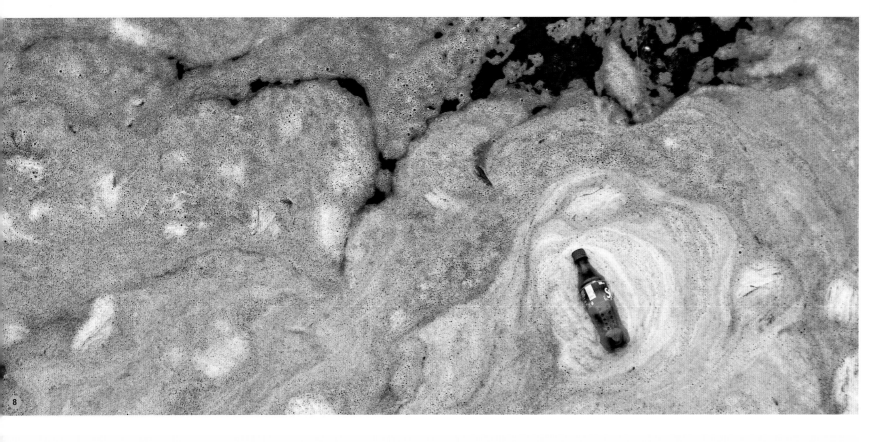

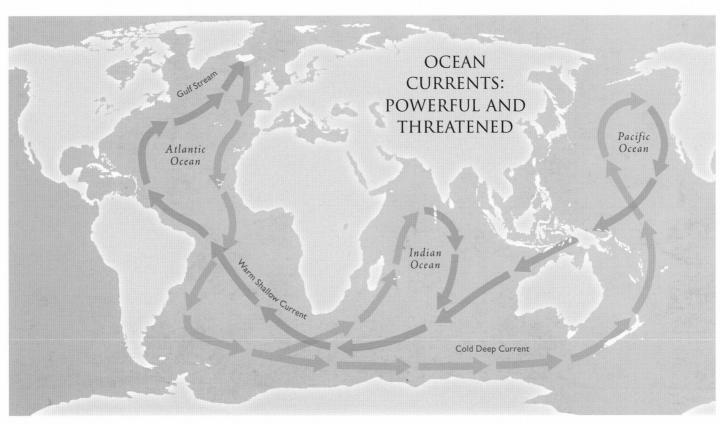

OCEAN CURRENTS: POWERFUL AND THREATENED

Gulf Stream

Atlantic Ocean

Pacific Ocean

Warm Shallow Current

Indian Ocean

Cold Deep Current

HOW CURRENTS WORK

1. Sun heats water in tropics

2. Water moves north, and gradually cools

North

3. Mixes with cold Arctic water and sinks

WHAT COULD WEAKEN THEM

1. Ice caps melt and rainfall increases due to global warming

2. Addition of fresh water makes North Atlantic less salty—therefore lighter—so it no longer sinks

3. Warm water can't move north

Picturing the Journey
PARTING SHOTS

The memories of circumnavigating North and South America remained vivid for the crew of *Ocean Watch* long after the journey was over. Not all of them were glamorous: days at sea are often long and tedious, and filled with chores and maintenance. But the hard miles were worth the effort, and the rewards—an undersea encounter, the wildlife and sunsets, the epic seascapes—were lasting images in the mind's eye.

Clockwise from opposite page, top left: Between watches, South American crewman Horacio Rosell caught some shut-eye despite boisterous seas. In heavy weather off Labrador, skipper Mark Schrader hung on for the ride. Before the voyage began, *Ocean Watch* underwent a complete refit. Once under way, Schrader practiced celestial navigation. On a scuba dive in the Galápagos Islands, author Herb McCormick signaled all was well.

Clockwise from above: In port, *Ocean Watch* proudly flew the banners of corporate backers Unilever and the Tiffany & Co. Foundation. High above the Arctic Circle, the crew encountered a pair of British Royal Marines voyaging in an open boat. In the Caribbean, the crew set sail southbound from St. Lucia. A polar bear and her cub in the Northwest Passage ice left an enduring impression.

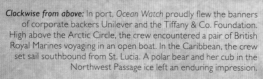

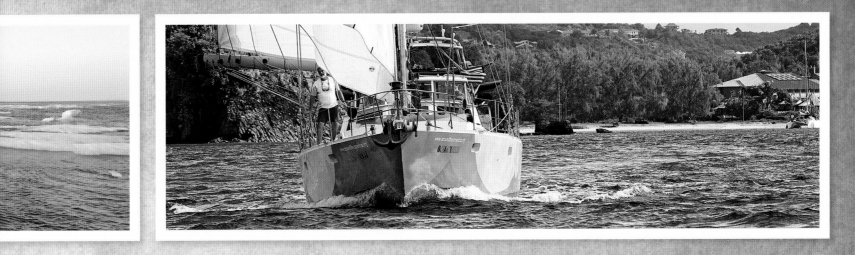

RESOURCES

Many organizations, websites, books, and other resources are available to those who want to learn more about the health of our oceans, those who wish to take action in addressing their health and well-being, or those who would like to grasp a broader understanding of nautical history and exploration. The following lists, institutions, tips, and bibliography can help you get started.

Organizations and Foundations

Sailors for the Sea
18 Market Square
Newport, RI 02840
(401) 846-8900
www.sailorsforthesea.org
Through numerous programs, projects, and initiatives, Sailors for the Sea—the ocean conservation group launched by David Rockefeller Jr. and David Treadway, and one of the founders and primary supporters of the Around the Americas expedition—enables individual boaters to educate themselves about ocean health and inspires them to become ocean stewards.

Pacific Science Center
200 2nd Avenue North
Seattle, WA 98109
(206) 443-2001
www.pacificsciencecenter.org
The Pacific Science Center (PSC) encourages "a lifelong interest in science, math, and technology by engaging diverse communities through interactive and innovative exhibits and programs." Along with Sailors for the Sea, the PSC was a major supporter of Around the Americas, developing a K–8 marine studies curriculum for teachers in English and Spanish (see www.aroundtheamericas.org). Educators from the center sailed aboard *Ocean Watch* and organized school visits and student tours throughout the expedition.

Algalita Marine Research Foundation
148 North Marina Drive
Long Beach, CA 90803-4601
(562) 598-4889
www.algalita.org
Founded by Charles Moore, who "discovered" the North Pacific Subtropical Gyre—also known as the Great Pacific Garbage Patch, or Trash Vortex—on a passage from Hawaii to California in 1997, the Algalita Marine Research Foundation has expanded its research worldwide, specifically focusing on the magnitude of our plastic "footprint," including the effects of fish ingestion of plastic on human health.

Applied Physics Laboratory
University of Washington
1013 NE 40th Street
Box 355640
Seattle, WA 98105-6698
(206) 543-1300
www.apl.washington.edu

The Applied Physics Laboratory of the University of Washington (APL-UW) was formed in 1943 at the request of the U.S. Navy to bring university resources to bear on urgent World War II defense problems. Now the school's "scientists and engineers make important contributions to understanding the Earth's climate cycles with satellite and *in situ* sensing of ocean winds, currents, and air-sea fluxes; observations of Arctic sea ice, its variations, and effects on mid-latitude oceans; and ocean tomography that reveals how the abyssal ocean mixes and sequesters carbon."

BoatU.S. Foundation for Boating Safety and Clean Water
880 South Pickett Street
Alexandria, VA 22304
(800) 245-2628
www.boatus.com/foundation
Through education and other projects, the foundation's goal is to be "the leader in boating safety and environmental education and outreach." Log on to the website and click on Clean Water Programs for a list of ideas, information, and action plans regarding recycling, fuel efficiency and alternative fuels, invasive species, algae blooms, and other related subjects.

California Academy of Sciences
55 Music Concourse Drive
Golden Gate Park
San Francisco, CA 94118
(415) 379-8000
www.calacademy.org
"The California Academy of Sciences is a multifaceted scientific institution committed to leading-edge research, to educational outreach, and to finding new and innovative ways to engage the public." The academy's remarkable 412,000-square-foot (38,276-sq-m) facility includes an aquarium, a planetarium, an expansive solar canopy, and an extensive water-reclamation system.

Fisheries and Marine Institute of Memorial University of Newfoundland
P.O. Box 4920
St. John's, Newfoundland
Canada A1C 5R3
(800) 563-5799
www.mi.mun.ca
Located on the edge of the Atlantic Ocean, the Marine Institute is recognized as one of the world's most respected centers for marine learning across multiple disciplines, from aquaculture, naval architecture, and marine engineering to nautical and environmental science. It operates two vessels for studies and testing.

Intrepid Sea, Air and Space Museum
Pier 86 (W. 46th Street and 12th Avenue)
New York, NY 10036-4103
(212) 245-0072 or (877) 957-7447
www.intrepidmuseum.org
The Intrepid Sea, Air and Space Museum is one of America's leading historic, cultural, and educational institutions. Located on the Hudson River aboard the aircraft carrier *Intrepid*, a National Historic Landmark, the museum is dedicated to promoting the awareness and understanding of history, science, and service through its collections, exhibitions, and programming.

Maritime Museum of the Atlantic
1675 Lower Water Street
Halifax, Nova Scotia
Canada B3J 1S3
(902) 424-7490
www.museum.gov.ns.ca/mmanew
The Maritime Museum of the Atlantic is Canada's oldest and largest such institution. "Visitors are introduced to the age of steamships, local small craft, the Royal Canadian and Merchant Navies, World War II convoys and The Battle of the Atlantic, the Halifax Explosion of 1917, and Nova Scotia's role in the aftermath of the *Titanic* disaster."

Maritime Museum of San Diego
1492 North Harbor Drive
San Diego, CA 92101
(619) 234-9153
www.sdmaritime.org
The Maritime Museum of San Diego "enjoys a worldwide reputation for excellence in restoring, maintaining, and operating historic vessels. The museum has one of the world's finest collections of historic ships." Ships are open for daily public tours—including the oldest active tall ship, the *Star of India*, built in 1863.

Monterey Bay Aquarium Foundation
886 Cannery Row
Monterey, CA 93940
(831) 648-4800
www.montereybayaquarium.org
The wondrous Monterey Bay Aquarium will captivate anyone who loves the ocean, but its website, educational programs and curriculums, and related resources are equally enthralling. The aquarium's Seafood Watch—which can be accessed online, in printed pocket guides, or on mobile devices—recommends which seafoods to buy or avoid, helping consumers and businesses become advocates for sustainable seafood.

New England Aquarium
1 Central Wharf
Boston, MA 02110
(617) 973-5200
www.neaq.org
"Founded in 1969, the New England Aquarium is a global leader in ocean exploration and marine conservation, combining education, entertainment, and action to address the most challenging problems facing the ocean. Through a wide variety of educational programs and conservation initiatives, [the aquarium's mission is to] make a lasting impact globally."

Oceana
1350 Connecticut Avenue, NW
5th Floor
Washington, DC 20036
(202) 833-3900 or (877) 762-3262
http://na.oceana.org
Employing science-based campaigns to achieve policy victories, with over 500,000 members, and offices in North America, Central America, South America, and Europe, Oceana is "the largest international organization working solely to protect the world's oceans." Since 2001, Oceana has protected more than 1.2 million square miles (3.1 million sq km) of ocean and countless sea creatures.

Plastic Pollution Coalition
2150 Allston Way, Suite 460
Berkeley, CA 94704
(510) 394-5772
http://plasticpollutioncoalition.org
"The Plastic Pollution Coalition is a global alliance of individuals, organizations, and businesses working together to stop plastic pollution and its toxic impacts on humans, animals, and the environment." Through education, networking, and political action, the alliance "seeks to put plastic pollution at the forefront of global social, environmental, and political discourse."

Reef Environmental and Education Foundation (REEF)
P. O. Box 246
98300 Overseas Highway
Key Largo, FL 33037
(305) 852-0030
www.reef.org
An active organization of divers and marine enthusiasts committed to ocean conservation, REEF was founded in 1990 as a way "to contribute to the understanding and protection of marine populations." The group achieves its aims through the REEF Fish Survey Project, which produces valuable information to scientists, marine park staff, and the general public.

Rosenstiel School of Marine and Atmospheric Science
University of Miami
4600 Rickenbacker Causeway
Miami, FL 33149-1098
(305) 421-4000
www.rsmas.miami.edu

Founded in the 1940s, the Rosenstiel School of Marine and Atmospheric Science is now regarded as one of the world's leading academic oceanographic and atmospheric research institutions. The main campus, on Florida's Virginia Key, "forms part of a specially designated 65-acre (26-ha) marine research and education park that includes two National Oceanic and Atmospheric Association laboratories, and a dedicated marine and science technology high school."

The Santa Barbara Maritime Museum
13 Harbor Way, Suite 190
Santa Barbara, CA 93109-2344
(805) 962-8404
www.sbmm.org
The Santa Barbara Maritime Museum preserves and celebrates the maritime heritage of the California coast and carries it forth via presentations, workshops, tours, and other programs. Located in the Santa Barbara Waterfront Center, the museum overlooks the Santa Barbara harbor and its flagship, the 1917 sportfishing yacht, *Ranger*.

Sea Education Association
P. O. Box 6
Woods Hole, MA 02543
(508) 540-3954
www.sea.edu
Since 1971 the Sea Education Association (SEA) has been a leader in off-campus study focused on marine science, maritime culture, and environmental studies. The SEA Semester study abroad programs (which take place aboard the 134-foot [41-m] brigantine, *Corwith Cramer*), challenge students intellectually and physically by combining sailing adventures around the world with study of the deep ocean and the interactions of humans and the sea.

Scripps Institution of Oceanography
U. C. San Diego
9500 Gilman Drive
La Jolla, CA 92093
(858) 534-3624
www.sio.ucsd.edu
"Scripps Institution of Oceanography is one of the world's oldest, largest, and most important centers for ocean and earth science research, education, and public service. Research at Scripps encompasses physical, chemical, biological, geological, and geophysical studies of the oceans and earth." The institute's Birch Aquarium provides the public with ocean science education, interprets research, and works to promote ocean conservation.

Shake-A-Leg Miami
2620 South Bayshore Drive
Coconut Grove, FL 33133
(305) 858-5550
www.shakealegmiami.org

Founded by Harry Horgan following an automobile accident that left him paralyzed, Shake-A-Leg Miami, on the shores of Biscayne Bay, is "one of the largest adaptive water sports facilities in the United States," serving people with disabilities, disadvantaged children and their families, and the entire South Florida community by integrating "education, recreation, health and wellness, and workforce training."

Surfrider Foundation
942 Calle Negocio, Suite 350
San Clemente, CA 92673
(949) 492-8170
www.surfrider.org
A grassroots organization founded in 1984 by a "handful of visionary surfers in Malibu, California, [the Surfrider Foundation] is dedicated to the protection and enjoyment of our world's oceans, waves, and beaches, and now maintains over fifty thousand members and ninety chapters worldwide." The organization's core campaigns fall under the following headings: Clean Water, Beach Access, Beach Preservation, and Protecting Special Places.

For Further Reading

The extensive, eclectic library aboard *Ocean Watch* included books on science, adventure, exploration, history, and the environment, as well as a wide range of fiction and classic novels ranging from Herman Melville's *Moby-Dick* to Yann Martel's *Life of Pi*. Here's a small sampling of the books we carried and used as reference volumes in our travels and studies (though some are out of print, all are available online), along with some important recent titles that have been published since the conclusion of our voyage:

Across the Top of the World: The Quest for the Northwest Passage, by James P. Delgado, Checkmark Books, 1999

While scores of books have been written about the Northwest Passage—including many first-person stories by the leaders of various expeditions—none of them are as all-encompassing as Delgado's wide-ranging and fascinating historical treatment. The rich assortment of maps, artwork, and photographs are equally unparalleled.

Arctic Dreams: Imagination and Desire in a Northern Landscape, by Barry Lopez, Vintage Books, 2001

The winner of the 1986 National Book Award, Lopez's lyrical narrative of his travels to Siberia, Greenland, and northern Canada—including his wondrous descriptions of the flora, fauna, wildlife, people, and landscapes—has been widely recognized (and deservedly so) as a modern classic.

1421: The Year China Discovered America by Gavin Menzies, Harper Perennial, 2004

This somewhat controversial book is based on a remarkable premise: in 1421, a huge armada set forth

from China to explore the world's oceans, calling not only in India and East Africa, but also in the Americas and Antarctica, centuries before European adventurers set foot on those continents. Menzies's research has been called into question, but one thing is certain: this is a fascinating, even rollicking, tale.

Over the Edge of the World: Magellan's Terrifying Circumnavigation of the Globe, by Laurence Bergreen, Harper Perennial, 2004

In 1519, Ferdinand Magellan and his fleet of five ships set sail from Spain in search of a water route to the Spice Islands of Indonesia. Three years later, the sole surviving vessel returned to Europe with just eighteen men; Magellan, killed in a fierce battle en route, was not among them. Bergreen's account of the unprecedented circumnavigation, and the discovery of the Magellan Strait, is compelling reading.

Seasick: Ocean Change and the Extinction of Life on Earth, by Alanna Mitchell, The University of Chicago Press, 2011

Veteran science journalist Mitchell earned the 2010 Grantham Prize for Excellence in Reporting on the Environment for this captivating—and troubling— examination of the planetary environmental crisis "through the lens of the ocean." Each chapter features a different group of researchers who introduce readers to significant concepts like the importance of ocean currents, the building of coral structures, the effects of acidification, and other topics.

Song for the Blue Ocean: Encounters Along the World's Coasts and Beneath the Seas by Carl Safina, Henry Holt & Company, 1998

The first of five books by Safina (a former commercial fisherman turned ecologist), *Song for the Blue Ocean*—a highly readable report of his travels and studies on the high seas, along salmon rivers, and among tropical

coral reefs—established the author as one of the most singular voices in contemporary marine conservation. His latest work, *A Sea in Flames*, scrutinizes the 2010 Deepwater Horizon oil spill in the Gulf of Mexico.

The Voyage of the Beagle, by Charles Darwin, Penguin Classics, 1989

A vivid travel memoir as well as a detailed scientific field journal, Darwin's lasting chronicle of his five-year survey expedition under the command of Captain Robert FitzRoy (originally published in 1839 as *Journal and Remarks*) laid the groundwork for his subsequent theories on evolution and natural selection.

The Wave: In Pursuit of the Rogues, Freaks, and Giants of the Ocean, by Susan Casey, Doubleday, 2010

Through the eyes of mariners, wave scientists, and extreme surfers, Casey's riveting examination of ocean waves also poses and answers a central question in the affirmative: will global warming lead to stormier oceans and bigger waves?

Weather Makers: The History and Future Impact of Climate Change, by Tim Flannery, Allen Lane, 2006

The author, a well-respected Australian scientist, avoids the hype and hysteria in this even-handed, authoritative, accessible investigation (Australia's Book of the Year in 2006) on the causes and implications of global climate change. The "weather makers," he concludes, are us, and we already possess the tools and knowledge to avoid cataclysmic changes to our planet.

Whales, Ice, and Men: The History of Whaling in the Western Arctic, by John R. Bockstoce, University of Washington Press, 1995

Arctic historian and archaeologist John Bockstoce has been traveling and working in the far north since 1962, and his well-researched, illustrative study of the rise

and fall of the whaling trade above the Arctic Circle provided insight and texture to our own travels through the Northwest Passage.

Taking Action

Aboard *Ocean Watch*, we kept a big supply of reusable bags on board for shopping and provisioning. You, too, can say farewell forever to plastic grocery bags. If enough of us do something small every day, particularly in what we consume on a regular basis, it will make a difference.

Here are a few little suggestions that can go a long way:

- Buy in bulk. Repackage in reusable containers.
- When on the water, toss nothing inorganic overboard.
- Bring your own mug to the coffee shop.
- Ride your bike.
- Cut the holes that might entrap marine life in plastic six-pack beer and soda ring holders.
- Don't buy single-serving bottles of water or other beverages.
- Filter tap water for drinking or purchase a water-maker for your boat.
- Recycle all plastics.
- Recycle old electronics, cameras, phones, MP3 players, laptops, GPS units, and so on. All major phone companies, as well as Best Buy and Office Depot, will recycle your old phone. Some websites (www.thinkrecycle.com, www.gazelle.com, www.myboneyard.com) will pay for certain used electronics in working condition.

Finally, pass the word: we're all in this together.

INDEX

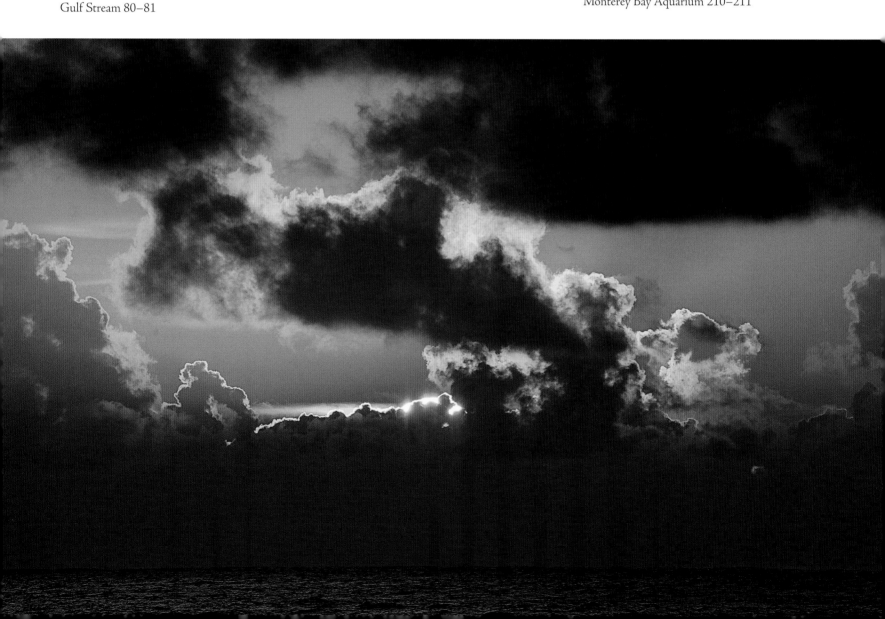

weldon**owen**

President, CEO Terry Newell
VP, Sales Amy Kaneko
VP, Publisher Roger Shaw
Executive Editor Mariah Bear
Editor Lucie Parker
Project Editor Amy Bauman
Production Editor Emelie Griffin
Creative Director Kelly Booth
Art Director and Designer Scott Erwert
Production Designer Michel Gadwa
Production Director Chris Hemesath
Production Manager Michelle Duggan

A WELDON OWEN PRODUCTION
© 2011 Weldon Owen Inc.

415 Jackson Street
San Francisco, CA 94111
www.wopublishing.com

Weldon Owen is a division of
BONNIER

Library of Congress Control Number
is on file with the publisher.

ISBN 13: 978-1-61628-171-7

ISBN 10: 1-61628-171-5

10 9 8 7 6 5 4 3 2

2014 2013 2012 2011

Printed by RR Donnelly in China

Produced in conjunction with

CRUISING WORLD

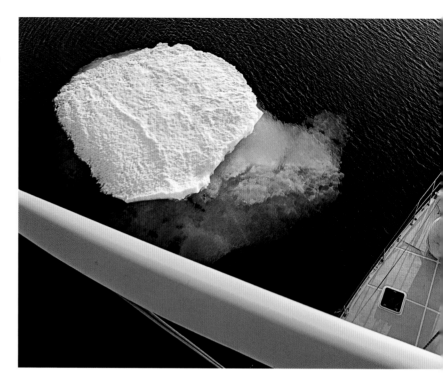

ACKNOWLEDGMENTS

FROM THE CREW OF OCEAN WATCH

It would take another entire book to fully recognize the institutions, supporters, family, and friends that made the Around the Americas expedition possible, but the crew of *Ocean Watch* would especially like to thank the following people, businesses, and organizations for their support.

Our principal partners were Sailors for the Sea (SFS) and Pacific Science Center (PSC), and we particularly wish to thank David Rockefeller Jr., David Treadway, Dan Pingaro, Chris Mancini, and Ned Cabot at SFS; and Bryce Seidl, Ellen Letvin, Erik Pihl, Kris Ludwig, Clayton DeFrate, Zeta Strickland, Roxanne Nanninga, Sara Bradshaw, and Stephanie Anderson at PSC. Thanks also to our shore-side team of Dawn Curtis Hanley, Bryan Reeves, Dan and Jane McConnell, Les Valsquire, Jim Lombardo, and Dr. Ray Jarris; the craftsmen who spearheaded the boat's refit, including Paul LaRussa, Andy Gregory, Jon Sebaska, Quinn Olson, Peter LaRussa, and Seattle's Seaview Boatyard; and Carol Hasse's loft of merry magicians at Port Townsend Sails.

The voyage would not have set sail without the generous contributions of our major underwriters—the Tiffany & Co. Foundation and Fernanda Kellogg, Unilever, the Rockefeller Family, the Osberg Family Trust, Osberg Construction, John and Gloria Osberg, Allen and Inger Osberg, and Grant and Patty Osberg—as well as our major supporters—James Bishop, Lacy Hoover and the Herbert W. Hoover Foundation, Charles Butt, the Campbell Foundation, John Castle, Jim and Dee Claypool, the Ettinger Foundation, Vantage in Philanthropy and David Guertin, Carl and Angela Sutter, and Jim and Nellie Kilroy.

Ocean Watch's scientific mission was a vast collaboration made possible by a wide range of institutes, scientists, and companies, including the University of Washington's Applied Physics Lab (Andy Jessup, Bill Asher, Jeff Simmen, Ignatius Rigor, and Craig McNeil); jellyfish expert Jennifer Purcell; the Joint Institute for the Study of the Atmosphere and Ocean (Tom Ackerman); the Martin-Fabert Foundation; the MIT Sea Grant Program; the National Oceanic and Atmospheric Administration (NOAA), which provided our Scientific Computer System (SCS), computer software, and special weather forecasts; National Aeronautics and Space Administration's (NASA) S'COOL Project (Lin Chambers); the Office of Naval Research; the International SeaKeepers Society, which provided our onboard thermosalinigraph; and Sea-Bird Electronics, which provided the Seacat probe we employed for our upper ocean survey along the Pacific Coast.

NASA's Alexander Smirnov deserves special recognition for his support and feedback on the Microtops sun observation program. And we're honored to acknowledge the scientists who accompanied us for portions of the trip: Michael Reynolds (who logged the most miles and became part of our core crew), Harry Stern, Warren Buck, Gretchen Hund Andrews, Peter Dahl, Axel Schweiger, and Applied Physics Lab engineer Dan Clark.

A remarkable roster of sailors also crewed aboard *Ocean Watch* (including many from Sailors for the Sea, Pacific Science Center, and our shore-side squad, already listed above) for several individual legs and became valued contributors to the team and truly enhanced our experiences under way. (Many of them were also our most important and missed supporters while they were ashore.) "Thanks" seems inadequate, but thank you, Rick Fleischman, William "Billy" Gannon, Carol and Peter Gluck, Tom Hoymer, Tyler Osberg, Jennifer Price, Ralph Schrader, Ed Stern, and Sam Treadway. A special *gracias* is in order for our best amigo, the wise and gentle Horacio Rosell, whose soul and seamanship (and Spanish!) helped guide us through Patagonia and around Cape Horn. And what can we say to our favorite shipmates—Maggie McCormick (at eleven years old, our youngest crew member), Kirsty Thoreson, and Joanna Wehrwein—except this: We love you. Thank you. We owe you. Big-time.

During our circumnavigation of the Americas, we enjoyed remarkable hospitality and/or advice and support from the Bruce family (Harry, Penny, Annabel, and Gabe), Dale Chihuly, Jim Rard, Bob Ross, Peter Hogg, Emily Feffer, Theresa Svancara, Steven Dahl, John Bockstoce, Craig George, Geoff Carroll, Wayne Thrasher, Peter Semotiuk, Glen Blackwood, Captain John Hughes, Lauren Curley, Mayor Joseph Riley (Charleston, SC), Brad and Meaghan Van Liew, Harry and Susie Horgan, Pablo Elola, Horacio Garcia Pastore, David and Candy Masters, Elaine Messer, Karen Neely, Alberto Mantellero, Mauricio Ojeda, Doonie Edwards, John Kenyon, Jaime Ackerman, Bill Walton, Emil Reutzell Jr., Hans Bernwall, Rob Moore, Manuel Maqueda, Fabien Cousteau, Tom Garnier, and Jay Platt.

The crew would also like to thank Sally Helme, Mark Pillsbury, and Elaine Lembo of *Cruising World* magazine; Eric Johnson and Eric Jensen of Seattle's KOMO-TV; John Castle, Steve Kennebeck, Kelly Meyer, and Tad and Joyce Lahman; and our marine industry and communication partners: Euro Marine Trading/Antal Marine Equipment/Lopo light, Fisheries Supply Company, Hatton Marine, Iridium Satellite Communications, Miller & Miller refrigeration, Northern Lights/Lugger Marine, Raymarine Instruments, Samson Rope, Ship's Medicine Chest/Lafferty's Pharmacy, Stratos Satellite Communications, Sure Marine Service, Winslow Life Raft, Helly Hansen, and Warren Light Craft.

Additionally, this book wouldn't have come together without the enthusiasm of and commitment by the San Francisco–based publishing house Weldon Owen, and particularly Terry Newell, Mariah Bear, Kelly Booth, and Grace Newell, and the outstanding design by Scott Erwert and the editorial contributions of Amy Bauman.

On a personal note, the crew would be more than remiss without mentioning our sincere thanks and affection to Michele Blockley and Richard Schrader; Tom Wallace, Jane Mauer, and Michael Thoreson; Nina and Bob McSparren; and Gail Carpenter.

Finally, we need to express our profound gratitude to the scores of people who followed us on the Web and visited *Ocean Watch* during her fifty-four stops in thirteen countries over the course of our thirteen-month, 25,524-nautical-mile voyage, especially the kids and students, to whom we dedicate this book. It turned out that the simplest, most straightforward lesson we learned in our travels was also the most profound: the children of the Americas are the future of our oceans.

FROM WELDON OWEN
Special thanks to Jacqueline Aaron, Meghan Hildebrand, Marisa Kwek, William Mack, Katharine Moore, Marianna Monaco, Michael Shannon, Marisa Solís, Charlie Wormhoudt, and Mary Zhang.

ART CREDITS
Diagrams of *Ocean Watch* by Conor Buckley, based on sketches by Gae Pilon
Map illustrations by Lohnes + Wright GIS and Mapping
Photo treatments and collaging by Scott Erwert

All photographs by David Thoreson, with the following exceptions:
Cover flap (Thoreson): Zeta Strickland 48 (left): Wikimedia Commons 53 (top left): Bryan Reeves 69 (bottom): Applied Physics Laboratory, University of Washington 81: Kristy Thoreson 88 (bottom right): Rick Fleischman 147: Alamy 138: Courtesy San Francisco Maritime NHP, J9 17,535 139: Courtesy San Francisco Maritime NHP, P91-003.50n 180 (bottom right): Mauricio Ojeda 220–221: Casey Woodrum